The Unusual Story of the Pocket Veto Case, 1926–1929

LANDMARK LAW CASES & AMERICAN SOCIETY

Peter Charles Hoffer
N. E. H. Hull
Williamjames Hull Hoffer
Series Editors

RECENT TITLES IN THE SERIES

Prigg v. Pennsylvania, H. Robert Baker

The Detroit School Busing Case, Joyce A. Baugh

Lizzie Borden on Trial, Joseph A. Conforti

The Japanese American Cases, Roger Daniels

Judging the Boy Scouts of America, Richard J. Ellis

Fighting Foreclosure, John A. Fliter and Derek S. Hoff

The Passenger Cases and the Commerce Clause, Tony A. Freyer

Discrediting the Red Scare, Robert Justin Goldstein

The Great Yazoo Lands Sale, Charles F. Hobson

The Free Press Crisis of 1800, Peter Charles Hoffer

Rutgers v. Waddington, Peter Charles Hoffer

The Woman Who Dared to Vote, N. E. H. Hull

Plessy v. Ferguson, Williamjames Hull Hoffer

The Tokyo Rose Case, Yasuhide Kawashima

Gitlow v. New York, Marc Lendler

Opposing Lincoln, Thomas C. Mackey

American by Birth, Carol Nackenoff and Julie Novkov

The Supreme Court and Tribal Gaming, Ralph A. Rossum

The 9/11 Terror Cases, Allan A. Ryan

Obscenity Rules, Whitney Strub

Speaking Freely, Philippa Strum

The Campaign Finance Cases, Melvin I. Urofsky

Race, Sex, and the Freedom to Marry, Peter Wallenstein

Bush v. Gore, 3rd expanded ed., Charles L. Zelden

For a complete list of titles in the series, go to www.kansaspress.ku.edu.

JONATHAN LURIE

The Unusual Story of the Pocket Veto Case, 1926–1929

UNIVERSITY PRESS OF KANSAS

Published by the University Press of Kansas (Lawrence, Kansas 66045), which was organized by the Kansas Board of Regents and is operated and funded by Emporia State University, Fort Hays State University, Kansas State University, Pittsburg State University, the University of Kansas, and Wichita State University.

Library of Congress Cataloging-in-Publication Data

Names: Lurie, Jonathan, 1939– author.
Title: The unusual story of the Pocket Veto Case, 1926–1929 / Jonathan Lurie.
Description: Lawrence, Kansas : University Press of Kansas, 2022. | Series: Landmark law cases and American society | Includes bibliographical references and index.
Identifiers: LCCN 2021050480
ISBN 9780700633395 (paperback) ISBN 9780700633401 (ebook)
Subjects: LCSH: Pocket veto—United States—Cases. | Indians of North America—Legal status, laws, etc.—Cases.
Classification: LCC KF5067 .L87 2022 | DDC 342.73/062—dc23/eng/20220208
LC record available at https://lccn.loc.gov/2021050480.

British Library Cataloguing-in-Publication Data is available.

Printed in the United States of America

10 9 8 7 6 5 4 3 2 1

The paper used in this publication is acid free and meets the minimum requirements of the American National Standard for Permanence of Paper for Printed Library Materials Z39.48-1992.

To our children,
and their children

Warning! History can lead to insight and may cause
increased awareness.
—Postcard in the Zeigeschichtliches Museum, Germany

CONTENTS

EDITORS' PREFACE

Jonathan Lurie's thorough, engaging, and persuasive account of the pocket veto case demonstrates how legal procedure, here the way in which the federal government chose to litigate Native American tribes' claims, trumped the substance of those claims. He brilliantly weaves two stories together—one beginning at the far western edge of the nation where Native peoples struggled to maintain their lands and customs, and the other ending in Washington, DC, where Congress, President Calvin Coolidge, and the Supreme Court had to, at least in theory, decide whether the Native people's claim had merit.

But that is not what happened. As Lurie warns the reader, "The pocket veto case well demonstrates the transformative power of the legal process." The book begins with a clear and convincing plea of the six tribes and ends with a decision that did not (spoiler alert) even mention the Native peoples or their land. Lurie opens the book, "Confident of their rights as litigants, the tribes—through their counsel—assumed that they would have what was commonly referred to as 'their day in court.' Thus they filed legal petitions that detailed the various alleged wrongs committed against them by the federal authorities." He concludes, "In the end, one of the interesting characteristics of my study is the total absence of the tribes as well as consideration of their claims from any of the judicial decisions analyzed therein. In terms of their legal significance, it is almost as if the six tribes did not exist."

There are heroes, for example, the Indians' counsel, William S. Lewis, and Congressmen Wesley Jones and Hatton Sumners, and there are, well, players for whom Lurie has little sympathy. Chief among these was President Calvin Coolidge. As the Native claims required special congressional approval, which they received, the only way that Coolidge, who had other views, could derail the process was the pocket veto. Legal histories of Native rights rarely have happy endings. This one is no exception. But that struggle goes on. So, too, in the other story, the "pocket veto case retains its relevance for ongoing legal issues concerning separation of powers—a never-ending source of constitutional friction."

Lurie's book shows a senior scholar's mastery of complex materials. With this work, we are again reminded of how valuable that skill is.

The perceptive reader will probably be curious about the word "unusual" as applied to a unanimous US Supreme Court decision rendered in 1929. Why does my account of this case, which affirmed as constitutional a practice utilized by presidents since the War of 1812, merit such a descriptive adjective? The answer to this question will, hopefully, be found in the following chapters. But it involves not so much the facts of the case as the factors that ultimately prompted six Native American tribes to file suit in the first place. The alleged grievances of the Colville, Lakes, Methow, Nespelem, Okanogan, and San Poil led them on a legal course that ultimately involved the US Congress, President Calvin Coolidge, and two federal courts.

Examination of the actual route that their case took follows herein. Confident of their rights as litigants, the tribes—through their counsel—assumed that they would have what was commonly referred to as "their day in court." Thus they filed legal petitions that detailed the various alleged wrongs committed against them by the federal authorities since the era of the Civil War. It becomes important, therefore, to understand both what these plaintiffs sought and why they felt justified in seeking redress, as these two factors formed the basis for their lawsuit. The Indians did indeed have their day in court, but not in the manner they had anticipated. Their claims were neither litigated nor resolved. Their grievances were in fact never argued, and instead a related legal issue wrapped around them resulted in the high court's unanimous decision. Indeed, with the exception of the case's title, *they* do not figure in what was supposed to be *their* case—hence the adjective "unusual" in the title of this book.

How did this case arise? In 1855 Congress had created a new federal court, the Court of Claims, a tribunal intended to provide a means whereby individuals might seek redress for wrongs against them allegedly committed by the federal government. Surely, if any group had such legitimate justification, it would seem to have been the Native Americans. Yet the 1855 statute made absolutely no mention of them. Further, when it expanded and strengthened the court in 1863, the legislature specifically barred this new tribunal from hearing any case "growing out of or dependent on any treaty stipulation entered into with foreign nations or with the Indian Tribes."

Such a restriction may not necessarily have been based solely on racial antipathy against Native Americans, as certain southern tribes actively supported the Confederate States. One can surely understand congressional resentment of such conduct in 1862–1863. Yet this restriction may also reflect the lasting influence of Chief Justice John Marshall, who had defined American Indians as "domestic, dependent nations." With the long-established legal doctrine of sovereign immunity in mind, foreign entities seeking to sue the United States could be expected to obtain some sort of authorization from Congress. Why not hold an Indian "Nation" to the same standard?

In the post–Civil War era and thereafter, this practice came to represent the basic reality for Indigenous peoples seeking redress against the United States. They had to obtain specific authorization from Congress—as well as presidential approval—in order even to appear before the Court of Claims, let alone prevail. In fact, efforts to gain such a statute represented a challenging and frequently unsuccessful route. The congressional process was time consuming (consider the distance between Washington State and the District of Columbia, for example) and expensive as well as unfair to tribes "with less clout." Nevertheless, by 1926 numerous tribes (there were more than five hundred of them in the United States) had procured the requisite special authorization from Congress, sometimes based on committee hearings, most typically by those dealing with Indian affairs. The six tribes just mentioned had gained, or so they thought, that all-important authorization, as well as hired an attorney. The road seemed clear for them to present their case against the United States. But roads sometimes have detours, as these chapters will reveal.

This study is divided into three parts. Part 1 includes three chapters, the first of which deals with the unique origins of the federal tribunal, which, in accordance with consistent decisions of Congress, appears to have been the only judicial body to which Indigenous tribes might apply for relief concerning claims against the United States. What factors had persuaded the Congress to establish a federal Court of Claims in 1855, and eight years later to expand its membership and strengthen its jurisdiction? What arguments were raised for and against its existence? Chapter

2 traces the paths taken both by the attorney for several of the six tribes, as well as by various congressional leaders as they moved toward enactment of that *sine qua non*, the special statute that would permit a lawsuit to be filed in the Court of Claims. What arguments were raised concerning the "rights" of the tribes to seek redress from the United States? How significant does their cause appear to have been to those members of Congress whose comments have been preserved in the *Congressional Record* and related materials? Finally, chapter 3 tracks the ultimate enactment of the special statute and its fate at the hands of President Calvin Coolidge. Famous as a chief executive who did little and said even less, has it been possible to extrapolate from available presidential papers any explanation for his decision to pocket veto the statute?

Part 2 also includes three chapters and focuses on the fate of the special bill at the hands of two federal courts—the Court of Claims and the US Supreme Court. Chapter 4 presents the points raised by counsel for the tribes, William Lewis, as he argued at some length for the legitimacy of his cause. What issues did he present, and how effective do they appear to have been for the judges of the Court of Claims, who joined in a unanimous opinion by Chief Judge Edward Campbell? Chapters 5 and 6 track the litigation as it headed to the Supreme Court. In terms of actual results, how effective were these final arguments offered by counsel in the case? Part 3 consists of two chapters: chapter 7 traces modifications of the pocket veto case after 1929, and a summary chapter brings my study to a close.

For their consistent encouragement, I am very grateful both to David Congdon of the University Press of Kansas and to Peter Hoffer, who suggested that my book belonged in the Press's Landmark Law Cases and American Society series. Thanks, too, to Kelly Chrisman Jacques, who shepherded it through production. A special word of thanks to the two readers who reviewed my manuscript for the Press. Their penetrating and perceptive observations were extremely beneficial as I undertook my final revisions. This book represents the fourth time I have been able to work with the Press, whose consistent support remains much appreciated. As has been true concerning a number of my books, these chapters have been read and critiqued by my good friend Melvin Urofsky. Again, I thank him for his comments, sometimes critical, but always accurate and encouraging. Several distinguished scholars in American

Indigenous history advised me during the early stages of this project. I am especially grateful to Philip Deloria, Alexandra Harmon, and David Treuer.

As has been true of a number of my other studies in legal history, the completion of this book would have been impossible without the ongoing support of the Library of Congress Manuscripts Division. Again I gratefully acknowledge the aid received from Jeff Flannery and his staff. This time around, Jeff guided me through the Calvin Coolidge Papers, which, as will be seen, are of critical importance to the first part of this book. The value of the LOC Manuscripts Division Reading Room to scholarly research cannot be overestimated.

Closer to home, for a number of years the reference librarians at Rutgers University have been virtually indispensable to my work. Again I thank Tom Glynn, whose uncanny ability to locate congressional reference sources remains remarkable. The assistance rendered by Stephanie Bartz and Rebecca Kunkel from the Rutgers Law School Library's Reference Department is gratefully acknowledged. Special thanks go to good friends Lorraine Williams and Richard Waldron, who tracked down some background information on Indigenous tribes within the state of Washington. Finally, I thank Mac, my foremost colleague, critic, friend, and gadfly whose persistence for more than fifty-two years has helped me bring this project to completion. Of course, I remain responsible for any errors that may lurk in these chapters.

PART I

The History of a New Federal Tribunal

CHAPTER I

The Long Road to the Court of Claims

One might expect that after a successful American Revolution, with the enumeration of multiple offenses allegedly committed by both the British Crown and Parliament against the colonies, set forth in the Declaration of Independence for all to read, the newly established United States would provide some means of redress for citizens claiming that they had been wronged by their government; all the more as the founding generation had not hesitated to reject out of hand the old British doctrine that "the king can do no wrong." In fact he could and did. By the revolutionary era, even the British legal system had provided for actions against the Crown. Indeed, one source recalls that George III asked a British jurist, "Why do I lose so many lawsuits in your court?" The judge supposedly replied, "Because Your Majesty is so often wrong."

Yet the original Constitution included no mention whatsoever of a right to pursue a claim against the federal government. Not until 1791, with ratification of the Bill of Rights, did the young federal government correct this omission. The First Amendment contains a provision forbidding Congress to make any law "abridging . . . the right of the people peaceably to assemble, and to petition the Government for a redress of grievances." Thus, as William Wiecek observed, in fact "the problem of claims against the central government antedated the Constitution," having originated during the years of the Confederation Congress. Moreover, he adds that multiple problems bedeviled official efforts to process them: "a lack of administrative machinery" as well as the utter absence of both a national judiciary and an independent executive. It is not surprising, therefore, that the Confederation Congress itself opted to take "sole responsibility for assessing the validity of claims against the United States." However, as later American history would repeatedly demonstrate, war "gave rise to an unusually high number of claims against the

Confederation," in this instance a result of the recent Revolutionary War. With possible reluctance but probable relief, Congress created "a quasi-executive three-man Board of Treasury, to which it shunted the flow of claims."

The inauguration of constitutional government in 1788 resulted in little significant change for the processing of claims until 1792, when Congress authorized widows and orphans of soldiers who had fought in the Revolution to press their claims for pensions, and further mandated that the new federal courts were to deal with them. But the statute "authorized the Secretary of War to suspend any judgments he found erroneous" and instructed him to report results to Congress. The resulting amalgam of congressional, executive, and judicial authority reflected an ongoing tension between the desire for "an independent claims tribunal" and Congress's retention of control over federal spending. Congressional inability to resolve these two goals would be an ongoing characteristic well reflected in future developments that led to the federal Court of Claims. Meanwhile, the number of claims continued to expand as the War of 1812 came and went.

Yet expansion did not result in increased resolution. By the time John Quincy Adams sat in Congress, the number of claims had "multiplied sevenfold" since his father had been president. Between 1831 and 1837, for example, more than fourteen thousand claims were presented to Congress. Only 5,891 received congressional attention, either favorable or unfavorable, while the remaining 8,811 "were not acted on at all." The former president was less than impressed. "There ought to be," he wrote, "no private claims business before Congress. There is a great defect in our institutions by the want of a Court of Exchequer or a Chamber of Accounts." It took the form of congressional inability to recognize that at bottom the matter of claims represented a legal issue. Adams insisted that "it is judicial business, and legislative assemblies ought to have nothing to do with it." Indeed, "a deliberative Assembly is the worst of all tribunals for the administration of justice." Half of the time of Congress "is consumed by it, and there is no common rule of justice for any two of the cases decided."

Adams's comments are contained in his diary, which extended to some twelve volumes and would not be published in his lifetime. Thus there is no way to ascertain how influential—although perceptive—his insights were. There is no doubt, however, that by the last years of his life (he died in 1848) Congress had been swamped with claims against the federal government. In response, it had established standing committees on claims in both the House and the Senate. Of course, the number of claims filed had burgeoned even as the United States expanded. Wiecek observed that by 1840 federal receipts totaled more than $19 million, while expenses had climbed to more than $24 million. The numbers of claims filed expanded as well. In the year when Adams died, the House Committee on Claims conceded that the "congressional procedures for claims adjudication" represented "a system of unparalleled injustice, and wholly discreditable to any civilized nation."

The question arises why Congress was so slow to respond to the problems inherent in its own system of resolving claims, all the more as it was well aware of them. Wiecek asserts, I think correctly, that the delay resulted from more than simple "conservatism or inertia." A section in Article I of the Constitution forbade drawing money from the Treasury except "in consequence of appropriations made by law." Therefore, he argues, "no court could issue an order binding on Congress for an appropriation." Yet the Constitution also guaranteed the right to petition. Between the desire of Congress to retain control of fiscal policy on the one hand, and the dilatory speed with which only a small minority of the claims were finalized on the other, the effectiveness of this constitutional right appeared minimal at best. A House committee observed in 1832 that "the right of petitioning Congress is the right of having petitions rejected."

"I want," exclaimed Mississippi representative Albert Brown in 1852, "something practical; something that will give the claimants justice; something that will protect the Treasury against fraud; keep the people's money under the control of the people's representatives, and at the same time relieve the Speaker's table from that accumulated and accumulating mass of private business under which it has literally groaned for five and twenty years." In fact, however, Brown's "wants" were "incompatible with each other," as Wiecek rightly observes. This background should be kept in mind as we turn to the establishment of the Court of Claims three years later, in 1855.

* * *

As first proposed by Pennsylvania senator Richard Brodhead, a commission would be established to examine and adjust private claims. But on being sent to a Senate committee, this proposal disappeared. In its place emerged a substitute bill that ultimately became the 1855 statute. It called for a three-judge Court of Claims, with its jurists to be appointed by the president, confirmed by the Senate, and granted life tenure—as is true of all federal judges appointed under Article III of the Constitution. Yet this new court differed from any other that Congress had created, and its enactment reflected the various incompatibilities that have already been noted. Signed into law on February 24, the new statute requires some discussion.

On first reading, the new tribunal appeared to have possessed a very broad purview. It shall "hear and determine *all* claims founded upon *any* law of Congress, or upon *any* regulation of an executive department, or upon *any* contract, express or implied with the government of the United States . . . and also *all* claims which may be referred to said court by either house of Congress" (emphasis added). The law further provided for appointment of a solicitor by the president, subject to Senate confirmation, to prepare and argue all cases on behalf of the United States, as well as commissioners to investigate the claims that had been filed. The judges could issue subpoenas, which "shall have the same force as if issued from a district court of the United State, and compliance therewith shall be compelled under such rules and orders as the court hereby created shall establish." Thus far the tribunal did not appear to be very different in basic structure from most federal courts. Yet the statute had not resolved the nagging questions of finality and force. What authority would back up the opinions handed down by the judges, and when could their decisions be considered final?

The answers appeared to be contained in section 7, where evidence of the unresolved issues mentioned above still lurked within its text. The statute mandated that the court "shall keep a record of its proceedings," and further, at the beginning of each session of Congress shall report to that body "the cases upon which they shall have finally acted, . . . with their opinion in the case, and the reasons upon which such opinion is founded." Moreover, the tribunal "shall prepare a bill or bills in those cases which shall have received the favorable decision thereof, in such form as, if enacted, will carry the same into effect." Thus, in addition to examining the various documents accompanying a claim and deciding on its merits or lack of same, the Court of Claims had to draft a bill reflecting its findings for submission to Congress, where, presumably, the legislators could act on it, decline to approve it, or do nothing. Apparently well familiar with the dilatory ways of Congress, the framers of the statute included a candid acknowledgment to that effect. "Said reports and the bills reported . . . shall, if not finally acted upon during the session of Congress to which the said reports are made, be continued from session to session, and from Congress to Congress, until the same shall be finally acted upon." On its own, in other words, the new Court of Claims possessed no authority to enforce its findings. Only Congress could do this. Were the reports from the court to be submitted to the entire House, or was Congress to consider each bill de novo? The House defeated a motion to refer the claims to the entire body of legislators.

Thus, decisions handed down could be implemented not by the court but by Congress. The legislation creating the Court of Claims in reality had created merely an advisory court for the legislative body. Such is not a conclusion from a legal historian reached with the benefit of historical hindsight but rather that of a contemporary critic. Four years after the court's founding, one observer remarked that "the system is a failure. No evil which led to the creation of the court is remedied." From 1855 to 1860, the writer added, "the Court had heard 224 cases and had given awards of over half a million dollars, but that Congress had passed acts to pay little more than half this amount, and this only after long delay." It would appear that for more than half a century Congress had been mired in uncertainty on the matter of claims, aware of the need for change, and willing to reform but apparently unwilling to give up its fiscal controls as effective reform would require.

While there may be a modicum of merit in this conclusion, in fact the 1855 statute contained the basic building blocks for a new and strengthened Court of Claims. Indeed, one lawyer arguing before it during the 1855 term insisted that the court should never forget that it was "the keeper of the nation's conscience." They remained in place when President Abraham Lincoln briefly turned to the subject in his first annual message to Congress in 1861. With prospects of a protracted civil war already in evidence by December of that year, Lincoln recognized that such a conflict "was bound to invite a massive number of claims as Union forces contracted for, damaged [and/or] destroyed a vast amount of private property." It became all the more important, therefore, that there be a legitimate and effective means for private claims against the Union to be equitably heard and decided, a process that would inspire public confidence in the federal government.

As a member of Congress, Lincoln had urged his colleagues to address the issue of claims. Now (December 3, 1861), eight months into his presidency, he returned to the subject, noting the need "for the adjustment of claims against the government, especially in view of their increased number by reason of the war." Lincoln reminded Congress that "it is as much the duty of government to render prompt justice against itself, in favor of citizens, as it is to administer the same between private individuals." Echoing John Quincy Adams, he insisted that "the investigation and adjudication of claims in their nature belongs to the judicial department." The president called the attention of Congress to the troubles confronting the federal authorities: "It is apparent that the attention of Congress will be more than usually engaged for some time to come, with great national questions." It had been intended by the organization of the Court of Claims—as Lincoln recalled—"mainly to remove this branch of business from the Halls of Congress."

Intimating that Congress had not yet succeeded in doing so, the president conceded that while the new court "has proved to be an effective and valuable means of investigation, it in great degree fails to effect the object of its creation, for want of power to make its judgment final." But Lincoln well understood the deep congressional divide concerning finality and the court. Although he chose his words carefully, there seems little doubt as to where he stood. "Fully aware of the delicacy . . . of the subject, I commend to your careful consideration whether this power of making judgments final may not properly be given to the court." He added, however, that the right of appeal to the Supreme Court should be reserved "with such other provisions as experience may have shown to be necessary." So Lincoln dropped, as it were, the issue of the Court of Claims back into the lap of Congress. Meanwhile, the war went on, ever expanding in scope, as the number of claims mounted.

Barely two months after receiving Lincoln's annual message, Indiana representative Albert Porter—for whom the future held election as governor of Indiana from 1881 to 1885—reported out a new bill dealing with the Court of Claims. Although it would take a little over a year, ultimately his bill, H.R. 226, became law. Unlike Lincoln, whom Porter quoted without identifying, he did not hesitate to chastise his colleagues. Congress "has often rejected just demands, and not unfrequently allowed unjust ones. It has failed to establish any uniform rules for its decisions." Even worse, "the time and attention to be devoted to great national interests have often been diverted to merely private claims." It is believed, Porter emphasized, that "no civilized nation, except our own, has failed to provide a tribunal in which justice can be done against the government." He might have added that the recently adopted Confederate Constitution included a "a provision that made it the duty of the Confederate Congress to create a court of claims for the Confederacy."

Porter conceded that Congress had already created a court of claims but in effect had rendered that tribunal impotent to enforce its findings. Now, he stated, "the best course that can be pursued is to reorganize the Court . . . and to place it on a basis on which it will be enabled to carry out the objects designed by its creators." Among the highlights of the bill, Porter noted two changes: (1) the court would be increased by two additional judges appointed in the same manner as were the first three in 1855; (2) in contrast to the original statute, members of either house of Congress "shall not practice in said court of claims." The scope of the revised Court of Claims was broad: "To the Court is given jurisdiction of all claims for which the government would be liable in law or equity were it liable to be sued in courts of justice." Moreover, Porter pointed to the fact that "its judgments are made final in all such cases," but provision was made for an appeal to the Supreme Court in any case where the "amounts involved exceed three thousand dollars."

Porter did not speak for a unanimous House committee. It is not clear how many disagreed with his majority report, but at least one congressman felt so strongly that he submitted a minority statement to accompany it, although only he signed the dissent. A single-term New York representative, Alexander Diven, argued that Porter's bill was both unnecessary and undesirable. It appears that he accepted the primary contention that some sort of tribunal to adjudicate claims was both necessary and legitimate, but not the one proposed by his colleague. Several of his points deserve brief mention. In the first place, under the current statute, the Court of Claims was required to submit proposed bills to Congress that would implement positive finding by the court. Further, "the testimony in each case is also to be transmitted. Thus it will be seen that this tribunal is admirably constituted to aid the government in determining the justice of claims made against [it]." Diven also objected to Porter's plan to increase the size of the court to five justices. "There is nothing satisfactory to show" that such a change is warranted. To be sure, there have been and remain numerous delays in resolving claims. But "the delay . . . arises from the omission of Congress to act upon the reports . . . rather than any delay before that tribunal." He insisted that "the law in regard to this tribunal can hardly be improved," and such improvement was not contained in Porter's bill.

Perhaps the relative rapidity with which the House acted on it can be explained by congressional awareness that the war was expanding on numerous fronts simultaneously—both military and financial—as was the number of claims submitted against the government. By the spring of 1862, any assumptions that this internecine conflict would be short and relatively bloodless had long since proved to be utterly inaccurate. All the more reason, therefore, that an effective and reputable means to adjudicate and resolve such matters should be available. On April 15 Porter called up the revised version of H.R. 226, and urged his colleagues to approve his measure. This time, he went into much greater detail than his earlier written statement for the committee.

Porter recalled that in contracts between the government and private parties, while the former "could resort to its courts to enforce the most minute provisions of every contract," when the latter sought redress for a breach, "however flagrant . . . , the courts were closed." Further, on turning to Congress for relief, all too often the claimant found "a body engrossed with public duties too important to allow a deliberate consideration of his claim, too numerous to hear and investigate it properly if desirous, bound by no judicial precedents securing uniformity of decision, and addicted to delaying for years decisions upon claims which a court would have readily disposed of in a day." Indeed, "caprice, commiseration, political partiality or prejudice, the popularity and tact of the member having a claim in charge, a sudden and hasty consideration of the question in a confused . . . House," all these "became elements . . . very frequently affecting the decision of claims."

Congressional awareness of these failings, insisted Porter, had resulted in the 1855 creation of the Court of Claims, replete with a stipulation "growing, perhaps, out of a pride which dislikes to part with the possession of power rather than upon any well-grounded reason has nearly destroyed the usefulness of the Court." His bill "makes out of the Court of Claims, which is now a mere commission, a court indeed, and relieves Congress of duties which . . . it has never been competent to perform." Yet Porter called attention to one additional provision in H.R. 226, a change that limited the authority of his newly strengthened tribunal and would be of major significance to future developments covered in these chapters.

"It will be observed," Porter stated, "that jurisdiction of claims arising upon treaties is withheld from the court." The 1855 statute had no such limitation. "According to the practice of nations, such claims are usually adjusted by commissioners especially appointed for the purpose. Besides, they often partake of a political character. . . . For these and other reasons it has been deemed prudent to retain the jurisdiction over them in Congress." None of his colleagues appear to have commented on this section. Moreover, when the Senate took up H.R. 226 in 1863, with no debate and not even a roll call vote, it added the words "or with the Indian tribes."

Congressman Diven appears to have been the only member of the House to speak against the bill, and his comments essentially reiterated what he had earlier written in his minority report. Several other members of Congress, both Democrat and Republican, voiced support for Porter's proposal. Examination of their comments indicates that by the spring of 1862, strengthening the Court of Claims was within congressional reach. Two examples may be cited. One is the comments of Ohio Republican John Bingham, for whom the future held not only authorship of section 1 of the Fourteenth Amendment but also a major role in the impeachment trial of President Andrew Johnson. The other is George Pendleton, a Democrat also from Ohio, who would be defeated for reelection in 1864 but would subsequently serve one term in the US Senate.

Bingham reminded his colleagues that the current Court of Claims was in fact not a court at all. In reality its members were but commissioners in chancery. "They can make no final decree or judgment of any kind." Any decision they ultimately reach is placed on the House calendar, "where its consideration takes up much of the time of the House, and subjects the Representatives of the people . . . to false and injurious imputations, whether they concur in the report or not. . . . It is a public scandal, and ought to be put an end to" [*sic*]. He added that there are approximately one hundred Court of Claims reports on the House calendar. Each will require time to consider. "Is an assembly of one hundred and eighty or two hundred Representatives . . . a fit tribunal calmly to consider and decide questions of fact and law touching on an individual's claim against the Government?" To ask the question was to answer it.

What Porter's bill did, according to Bingham, was simply to enable a citizen to transfer his claim from Congress "to a tribunal where his claim can be calmly and considerately examined, and be passed upon according to law and equity." No US citizen can complain of that. The simple question facing the House "is whether we will grant this privilege . . . or whether we will retain the old system, and allow the citizen to get along the best way he can, to the infinite disgust of the community at large, and the disgrace of the Representatives of the people." Indeed, "in my judgment, a wiser or more necessary act of legislation touching the interests of the people of the country has not been presented to this House."

John Hickman, a Republican from Pennsylvania, expanded on Bingham's position. Porter's bill "relieves Congress of the determination of these questions which it cannot rightly, or properly, or knowingly determine." Further, it gives judicial determination to the claims. "They are not made to depend upon the whim, or caprice, or friendship, or ignorance of members of this House, as they are now." Hickman exclaimed, "There is hardly a case so bad that it may not be carried in a court of law if the court only hears one side of the case; and it is very seldom that a committee of this House hears both sides of any claim."

George Pendleton rebutted Diven's insistence that Porter's changes were not necessary because the government is always prepared to undertake that which equity and justice require it to do. "That is very good in theory, but it is very bad in practice." Indeed, can any congressman "pretend to say that he himself can undertake justly, honestly, and fairly to administer the law between every applicant for justice and the Government?" Concerning the one hundred or so claims now pending in the House, can any congressman insist that "he has himself investigated the cases, and understands them so thoroughly that he could do justice or anything like justice in his vote on them?" Again, as with John Bingham's earlier comments, to ask the question was to answer it. Pendleton described the current process of claims resolution as "a course of conduct which would disgrace any individual in the eyes of the community in which he lives."

Pendleton's remarks reflected a tone of hostility toward government expansion of authority and power taken by many Democrats in Congress during the Civil War era. "What is the Government?" he asked. "It is constituted as this Congress is constituted, [and] composed of men not a whit more intelligent, or more laborious, or more painstaking, or more disposed to do justice than ourselves." Its obligations should be enforced as rigorously as are obligations of the citizenry to one another. Pendleton was "in favor of subjecting the Government to the same rigid discipline in the administration of justice to which I would subject an individual." What if the government was deleterious or even failed to pay on a claim as ordered? Pendleton had a ready answer.

[I] would authorize claimant to levy upon the property of the United States. I would have the post offices, the custom houses, and the court houses levied upon and sold to satisfy the judgment. I would sell here in the city of Washington those vacant squares fronting on the avenues. I would sell these desks and tables and chairs, if necessary, before I would see a man, whose claim was decided to be just and right and fair, forced to be a humble suppliant for justice at the hands of Congress. Either make this thing complete, or do away with it altogether. . . . Whenever the Government shall fail to do its duty, to make provision for the payment of every claim which has been solemnly adjudged to be good, I am willing to subject its property, as the property of the individual, to execution and sale.

At least one member of Congress may well have considered Pendleton's position too extreme and sought clarification from him. Would the future Indiana senator, asked Hendrik Wright—a fellow Democrat from Pennsylvania—"expose the military property of the Government to sale and execution? Does [he] contemplate the seizure and sale of the artillery and other munitions of war . . . to satisfy the claims of claimants. and thus leave the Government defenseless?" Pendleton apparently was unfazed by the question. "So long as there was plenty of other property, there would be no necessity of seizing on the military stores of the Government." But Wright and the rest of the House should understand that "when the Government cannot or will not pay its citizens what it owes them, under the decisions of a judicial tribunal, I am in favor of sacrificing cannon or any other property of the United States, if necessary, in order to satisfy these just claims."

Yet he went further: "I am opposed to the dogma, which has no foundation in justice, that the Government ought not be sued." Such a policy represented "a mistake from the time it was inaugurated up to this hour." Indeed, Pendleton supported Porter's measure "because it makes the Government suable, and when the Government is made suable, I would also make it liable to execution." Moreover, "I would apply the same rule to the Government that I would apply to individuals, and I would subject them and their interests to the adjudication of the same tribunal," and finally, "I would execute their decisions against the Government in exactly the same mode—as certainly, as rapidly—as I would execute their decision against the citizen and in favor of the Government." Pendleton was the last speaker to offer substantive comment on H.R. 226, which—with the addition of one amendment—passed the House by voice vote. The amendment simply required assurance that a successful claimant had not voluntarily aided or given encouragement to rebellion against the Union. Thus, on April 15, 1862, the Porter bill headed for the US Senate, where it was promptly referred to the Judiciary Committee. Not until December did that body report a heavily amended version to the full Senate, and on January 12, 1863, the Senate began debate on the measure.

*   *   *

Unlike the House, which managed to debate, discuss, and decide H.R. 226 in one sitting, the Senate—as was its wont—took its time. For the most part, consideration over a two-month period was desultory, and it revealed deep-seated differences among senators concerning not only the validity of the bill but also its very necessity. When Lyman Trumbull, a Democrat from Michigan and currently at the start of what would be a ten-year term as chairman of the Senate Judiciary Committee, moved that his colleagues postpone all other pending business to take up the Court of Claims bill, he was met with determined opposition from

John Hale, Republican from New Hampshire, described in demeanor as "black as Ink—Bitter as Hell." Voicing the equivalent of a "hell no!" response, Hale would have none of it.

Now was not the time, Hale insisted, to discuss such a bill, about which "I do not know anything." In truth, "the national life is trembling in the balance today, and I think we have something else do besides passing . . . Court of Claims bills." "As for myself," he fulminated, "I have no desire, I have no heart, I have no feeling for any legislation that does not look to the salvation of the country. Sir, it is time we woke up; it is time we looked our condition straight in the face; and I think when we do that, if we understand and appreciate that condition, our thoughts will be turned on something besides [the] Court of Claims."

Trumbull appears to have been familiar with Hale as a colleague and less than inspired by him as a speaker. If the senator from New Hampshire had a specific proposal pending that concerned Union armies in the field or could assist in crushing the rebellion, Trumbull would be glad to put H.R. 226 aside. But there "appears to be no measure of that kind at this moment pressing upon the Senate." As to the Court of Claims, it was time to fish or cut bait. The court "should either be abolished or it should be organized on a different footing—one or the other—and I have no great partiality as to what course shall be pursued in reference to it." Indeed, "I have no feeling in regard to this bill at all." Such averment to one side, Trumbull went out of his way to facilitate Senate passage of this measure.

As currently constituted, however, Trumbull considered the court to be only "an excrescence upon the Government; its judgments amount to nothing," and "we had better dispense with that court . . . or else give some effect to the decisions it makes." Echoing John Quincy Adams, who had made a similar point some thirty years before, he added, "I think the worst place in the world to pass upon claims against the Government is in Congress . . . [and] it has become notorious in the country that a bad claim is about as likely to pass through Congress as a good one." Hale insisted that the decision to give finality to the Court of Claims decisions "surrenders the constitutional prerogative to this court. I shall vote against [it] first and last, early and late, if I vote alone or in a crowd . . . and I hope the Senate will not take it up." It did, only to set the measure aside to consider other matters.

Two days later, the Senate again turned to H.R. 226 with a more extensive debate. Again Lyman Trumbull spoke on the measure, one that already "has been considered with very considerable care. It is not one of first impression." On the contrary, it passed the House and had been reported out from the Committee on the Judiciary. Indeed, Trumbull insisted, "no bill which has been before that committee has received more careful consideration than this." Now he supported amending the law, as proposed by his committee. But he added a caveat that if his colleagues determined to postpone the bill indefinitely, Trumbull would vote for a proposal to "abolish the court as present[ly] organized."

Maine Republican William Pitt Fessenden, for whom the future held both a short tenure as Lincoln's last secretary of the treasury and a leading role in the preparation of the Fourteenth Amendment, lauded the accomplishments of the Court of Claims during its eight-year history. To be sure, there had been delays in implementing many of its findings. But that "is not the fault of the C[ourt] of C[laims]." Rather, "it is because . . . Congress has failed to do its duty with regard to these claims, and has not acted upon them as speedily as justice required." Even with this concession, however, Fessenden had a more fundamental objection to Trumbull's bill.

In spite of the fact that members could be found in Congress "who are as competent to judge as any court that we should be likely to establish," H.R. 226 "proposes to give away the whole jurisdiction and power of Congress over claims against the Government, and lay the United States Treasury at the feet of a court outside." In my judgment, he added, "it would be utterly unsafe for us to part with the power of finally adjudicating upon claims against this Government." The fact that it does this "is so exceedingly dangerous . . . that I am ready to dispose of the bill now," by supporting Senator Hale's motion to postpone indefinitely, a motion that was still awaiting a formal tally of the yeas and nays. Fessenden's concern reflected the lingering unwillingness in the Senate to resolve the issue of finality for Court of Claims decisions, and he was not yet finished with H.R. 226.

In the meantime, the Senate considered and ultimately adopted with minimal—if any—debate approximately one dozen amendments to the original House bill, as drafted by Trumbull's committee. Several of them should be noted. As originally passed by the House, the Porter bill stipulated that the Court of Claims "shall have the jurisdiction of all claims for which the government would be liable in law or equity if it were suable in courts of justice." In its final form, the statute provided "for the satisfaction of private claims against the Government founded upon any law of Congress, or upon any regulation of an executive department, or upon any contract express or implied." It will further be recalled that the Porter bill excluded from the purview of the Court of Claims any claim dependent on any "treaty stipulation entered into with foreign nations." With no discussion whatsoever, and without a recorded vote, the Senate accepted the addition of five more words to this section: "or with the Indian tribes." Specific congressional authorization would now be required if an American tribe sought access to the Court of Claims. How can such a significant addition to the 1863 statute be explained?

One reason may well lie in the fact that by 1863, Congress was aware that certain of the southern Native "Nations" had allied themselves with the Confederacy. Indeed, it will be recalled that the House had previously adopted the Shellabarger Amendment (as would the Senate) to Porter's bill. Further, a well-regarded legal canon of sovereign immunity held that normally there had to be some sort of legislative enactment permitting a government to be sued by another foreign government. Since the days of Chief Justice John Marshall, the term "nation" had been applied to Indigenous American tribes. Members of Congress may have concluded that it was not unreasonable to hold Indigenous tribes to a similar standard. Finally, Congress could not have been immune to long-standing American hostility toward the Indigenous tribes over the last century. Whatever the explanation, however, there is no doubt that these five words were of major significance, in spite of the total lack of interest, discussion, and even a recorded vote.

For the last thirty years, members of Congress had declaimed against the unsuitability of that body to investigate and resolve private claims. They had offered cogent reasons as to why this was the case. Indeed, progress toward an enlarged and strengthened Court of Claims had been heralded as an appropriate and effective solution to the problem. By barring the tribes from its coverage in the absence of a specific congressional mandate, however, the legislature placed them in a position similar to—if not worse than—that which had confronted other private complainants prior to 1863. If the legislation made it easier for a great majority of such plaintiffs, the amended statute made it all the more difficult for the tribes to gain judicial relief. Can this exclusion be described as a typical example of American antagonism toward the Indigenous tribes?

In the meantime, with the amendments proposed by the Judiciary Committee still pending, Ohio senator John Sherman echoed William Fessenden in urging that now (January 1863) was not the time to take up this bill. "We must provide for a general conscription law. It is idle for us to avoid the necessity for it." Further, "we must provide for the payment of the soldiers, for the payment of the public debt, and for maintaining the public credit." All seemed of far greater importance to Sherman than the Court of Claims bill. Indeed, "no great harm can result from allowing the present court . . . to go on as it has for some years." He proposed postponement of all questions, if possible, "not intimately connected with the prosecution of the war. . . . Upon that prosecution depends not only our property but our lives; everything is at stake."

Senator Lazarus Powell, a single-term Democrat from Kentucky, urged that the bill be passed. He paid his respects to Senator Hale as one "who seems to have a penchant for assaulting courts." He reminded his colleagues, as had Trumbull, that "of all the tribunals on the earth, Congress was the least adapted to give a fair adjudication of a claim." Indeed, "my experience here is, that if a claim is large, old, and stale, it has a better opportunity to pass than if it were of another description." By a recorded roll call vote of eleven yeas and twenty-nine nays, the Senate declined the indefinite postponement of Trumbull's bill.

At that point Fessenden moved an amendment that, as he put it, would "test the question whether the Senate is disposed to place in the hands of the court the power to render final judgments against the United States." A vote against his amendment meant rejection of the finality for Court of Claims decisions. Not surprisingly, Senator Hale strongly supported his colleague. He pontificated,

I hope that when some future Gibbon shall write the history of the rise and fall of the great Republic, and shall give the indications which marked its progress to decay, one of them will be that [in 1863] the 37th Congress took it into their head that they were wiser than anybody that went before them, and departed from all the precedents established by their fathers, and started out on new, untried, and extravagant theories and notions.

For Hale, one of the worst such efforts was this misguided effort to give finality to Court of Claims decisions.

> You propose to vest this court with power that you have denied to the highest courts in the land. It is to me a tendency full of evil import. . . . I think, sir, if we were ever to have such a law, that this of all times and of all occasions is the worst and the most fatal; and I do hope that this feature of it will not pass. Do anything else but do not do this. Let us at least hold onto this.

James McDougall, a one-term Democrat from California, responded that he "should like to have some senator show me how committees of the two Houses of Congress will prove better and more careful judges of the rights of both parties than courts organized for that very purpose. The business of all courts is the administration of justice. But the manner in which business is transacted here is a denial of justice to citizens."

Possibly seeing nothing to be gained from further debate, Fessenden called for the yeas and nays on his amendment. The closeness of the vote indicated that the Senate remained divided over the issue of finality for the Court of Claims decisions. Indeed, the roll call could not have been closer. It resulted in a 20–20 tie, and Vice President Hannibal Hamlin cast the deciding vote against the amendment, meaning that the element of finality would remain attached to the bill as had been the case with the original measure from Congressman Porter. After a few futile attempts to delete the essence of the Shellabarger Amendment from Trumbull's bill, the Senate moved on to other matters. H.R. 226 remained stalled.

Examination of the *Congressional Globe* makes it clear that by January 19, 1863, a core of senators were unified in their opposition to the consideration of Trumbull's bill. They included William Pitt Fessenden, Republican from Maine; John Hale, Republican from New Hampshire; James Grimes and James Harlan, both Republicans from Iowa; and John Sherman, Republican from Ohio. Fessenden and Sherman appear to have objected less to the bill in principle than to the timing of its consideration. Lyman Trumbull, who had presented the bill from his Judiciary Committee, found the continual delay frustrating. Already the bill had been "very considerably discussed; and the Senate is in a better condition to consider it now than it will be a week hence. . . . I think we ought to have done with this bill, but the longer we delay taking it up the longer time it will occupy." Hale responded by noting that "it shall never be my reproach that when there were but about thirty days of the session left, those days were frittered away by considering bills of this character." Although the Senate agreed by a vote of 25–11 to take up the bill, after inconsequential debate it was set aside once again.

When the Senate reconvened a day later, yet again Trumbull moved to take up his bill. This time John Sherman insisted on a call for the yeas and nays. "I desire," he said, "to impress upon the Senate, if I can, the importance of laying aside all these mere legislative bills that are of no great importance." In truth, he insisted, the Senate had better things to do with its time. Bills setting up conscription, reorganizing the army, and providing for the credit of the government all required prompt attention. Yet "we waste the time of the Senate on a bill of no practical importance, even if it is adopted, when measures of most vital importance press upon us day by day. . . . What difference does it make whether there be three or five judges in the Court of Claims . . . ? We ought," maintained Sherman, to "lay aside this class of legislation entirely. Let us allow peace to dawn upon this country before we appropriate any more money for the establishment of courts of claims, or for the payment of old claims that date back in the history of this Government to its foundation. Let us lay aside all these collateral questions, which are totally unimportant." His eloquence not withstanding, by a vote of 23–13 the Senate took up H.R. 226 once more.

The resulting debate was desultory and inconclusive, until Senator Grimes spoke about his proposed amendment that would not only delete the entire bill but substitute in its place a brief sentence abolishing the Court of Claims. The basis for his opposition appears to have been his lingering concern over the finality of the court decisions. Grimes would "rather go back and stand where we were in 1855 before it was established, than to progress under the direction and influence of [Senator Trumbull], and give . . . extraordinary jurisdiction to tribunal." But the Iowa Republican did "not expect that [my] proposition . . . will be adopted. I fancy I can see where this thing is about to lead." W. Pitt

Fessenden from Maine added, "I see an apparent determination to pass the bill." Thus he would support Senator Grimes.

Both Grimes and Fessenden were prescient in predicting the future, albeit not immediately. Without warning, Lafayette Foster, a Republican from Connecticut, brought Senate proceedings to a sudden halt. "We have been engaged upon this bill for almost three hours," he observed, yet "we are further from the question upon its passage than we were when we began." He moved to table the bill, thus cutting off further discussion, and further moved for a vote on the yeas and nays. The vote was promptly taken and "shows the Senate to be without a quorum." Immediately Hale moved to adjourn, and Trumbull called for the yeas and nays yet again. The Senate overwhelmingly rejected Hale's motion, but "this division still shows the want of a quorum."

At that point, the Senate passed a motion that "the Sergeant at Arms be directed to request the attendance of absent members." Jacob Collamer, a Republican from Vermont, objected, asking, "Is anything to be gained by that course? Are we to stay here until [he] goes out into the city and invites members to come in?" I would rather, he added, "he doing something here besides waiting." He criticized his absent colleagues who chose "to stop the business of the country. Let them understand that we had to go home on account of their absence, and then see if they will hereafter absent themselves." Collamer protested against such conduct, "and I move that the Senate adjourn." It did.

*   *   *

It turned out that January 21, 1863, would be a decisive day in the history of H.R. 226. Shortly after the Senate reconvened, Trumbull reminded his colleagues about the measure. With two roll calls pending, it had stalled due to lack of a quorum on January 20. With no debate, the Senate declined to table the bill, by a vote of fifteen to twenty. The proposal from Senator Grimes met a similar fate by a vote of 11–25. After acceptance by Senator Trumbull of a few more minor amendments, Vice President Hamlin ordered the bill as amended to be reported to the full Senate. What had earlier transpired while the Senate met as a Committee of the Whole now had to be ratified all over again by the same body. The great majority of the amendments adopted earlier were accepted with no discussion. Fessenden, Hale, and Sherman, however, sought to delay if not prevent what they conceded to be its inevitable passage. This was the last opportunity for Senators to weigh in on H.R. 226.

Early in the debate, by voice vote the Senate mandated that all private claims for which the government would ordinarily be liable were to be referred directly to the Court of Claims "as a matter of course without a vote of the Senate." There remained, however, a significant exception to this provision, one of great relevance for developments to be discussed in later chapters of this study. The exception referred to claims "unless otherwise ordered by resolution of the House in which the same are presented or introduced." This proviso ensured that Congress could still have a role in selecting what cases would be heard by the court. Senator John Sherman proposed an amendment that would have given Congress even greater control over the tribunal. Certain claims allowed by the court "shall be submitted to Congress, and shall not be paid unless specific appropriation shall be made there for."

Sherman insisted that without some restraint imposed on the Court of Claims judges concerning payment of "old and antiquated claims, you will have gathered around the Court of Claims a set of harpies more violent more persevering than all those who have surrounded the lobbies of this Congress." All the lobby agents of the country "will gather around that tribunal. The judges are liable to be deceived, liable to be misled, liable to be corrupted." Lyman Trumbull responded that Sherman was raising the "old question over again, and it has been reiterated here time and time again. . . . Now, if the repetition and the reiteration time and again of this assertion can make it so, it will be so." But Sherman was not alone in his opposition to H.R. 226.

James Harlan, a Republican from Kansas, added, "I see no necessity for the bill." He asserted that in his opinion, "none of us are infallible," and judges "are as liable to err as Senators." Harlan did not see that any court of claims, "however constituted, would be as safe a tribunal to hold the purse-strings of the nation as Congress itself," and "none would be more just to claimants themselves." By January 21, H.R. 226 had been taken up only to be laid aside multiple times in the Senate, and senators were getting restive.

William Pitt Fessenden reminded his colleagues that "there has been a very considerable quantity of unnecessary noise." Fessenden was not alone in his use of sharp comments. New Hampshire Republican John Hale informed the Senate that Lyman Trumbull "is very impatient, I know, under anybody's speeches, except his own." If Sherman was determined to prevent the Court of Claims from having what he feared was unlimited control over the amounts it could award, Pitt Fessenden was equally determined to block the court's judgments from being "final." With debate winding down, yeas and nays were demanded for each of these issues with very similar results. Sherman's amendment lost by only a three-vote margin, 18–21. Although the court's later history would prove his fears to be unfounded, in 1863 they were apparently shared by a number of Sherman's colleagues. Fessenden's amendment, which simply would have stripped the court of any finality concerning its decisions, went down to defeat by a larger margin, 16–23. Although the last amendment considered by the Senate restored the number of judges on the Court of Claims to three by vote of 21–17, the change would be short lived. (Ultimately congressional conferees reinstated Porter's original language to include two additional judges.) By the same identical margin by which the Senate had defeated Fessenden's earlier amendment, on his new motion to call for the yeas and nays on final passage of the bill, it passed by a vote of 23–16. After the inevitable joint congressional committee recommended the final changes necessary to unify the two different bills, without discussion both chambers accepted the committee's report, and President Lincoln signed the bill into law on March 3, 1863.

By way of summary, several points can be reiterated. In the first place, a number of senators exemplified by Sherman and Hale insisted that passage of the measure to expand and strengthen the Court of Claims was not urgent, even if desirable. It did not represent a high priority. Indeed, examination of the measures relevant to the ongoing war that were enacted into law during the Thirty-Seventh Congress lends some credence to their point. Among other things, by the spring of 1863 it had passed the Homestead Land Grant Act, the Morrill Act, the first Confiscation Act, the Pacific Railroad Bill, a tariff measure, and the abolition of slavery in the District of Columbia, to say nothing of all the war-related measures needed to create, fund, maintain, supply, and compensate what would become the largest American military force thus far in our history. Compared to such significant legislative landmarks, adding two more judges to the Court of Claims did not seem of great moment. Further, two key components of Porter's original bill survived senatorial vicissitudes to become law. The Court of Claims gained finality for its decisions, although they could still be appealed to the US Supreme Court, and with one important exception Congress was essentially removed from referring claims cases to it. There would be no further special appropriations to fund specific court decisions.

Moreover, although the Senate added the words "or with the Indian tribes" to the section of the statute that limited court jurisdiction, this author could find no mention whatsoever of any form of explanation why the Senate took such a step and why the House acquiesced. Nor in either chamber does there appear to be a single word of discussion about this exclusion. Some possible explanations for such omission were mentioned earlier in this chapter and need not be repeated here. Thus there can be no doubt that on its face, the statute barred the Court of Claims from deciding any cases brought by the Indigenous tribes. But section 2 of the statute apparently mitigated the specific exclusion found in section 9. It provided that all petitions and bills that concerned private claims against the government (barring the exclusion in section 9) "shall be transmitted" to the court by the appropriate officials of either the House or the Senate, "unless otherwise ordered by resolution of the House in which the same are presented or introduced." In other words, by specific mandate Congress could authorize a tribe to raise a case before the Court of Claims.

Thus the argument that Congress never intended this amended statute to apply to claims brought by the Indigenous tribes becomes irrelevant. To be sure, the law made it much more difficult for them to gain its benefits than other Americans seeking redress against the government. But if a tribe could secure congressional passage of a special act authorizing it to sue in the Court of Claims, the way would be open to gain redress from that tribunal—a difficult but by no means impossible route to follow. Numerous tribes would attempt to do so. Eighteen years after Porter's bill became law, and "apparently tiring of its efforts to square accounts between the federal government and Indian tribes, Congress in 1881 passed the first special jurisdictional act, authorizing the Court of

Claims to adjudicate differences between the federal government" and specified tribes.

Between 1881 and 1926 over one hundred such statutes appear to have been enacted. All that was needed, apparently, were specific authorization from Congress, supposedly founded on legitimate grounds for complaint, and an attorney to handle the case before a federal tribunal especially created to resolve claims against the government. By 1925 a group of Indian tribes in the state of Washington had hired such an attorney and assumed—not unreasonably—that the way was open for enactment of the requisite statute by Congress. The outcome is discussed in the following chapters. To paraphrase the poet Robert Burns, however, the best laid plans of mice and men oft gang after gley, and leave us nought but grief and pain for promised joy.

CHAPTER 2

Approaching the Gates of the Court
The Six Tribes and Congress until 1927

In 1872 President Ulysses S. Grant issued an executive order that established an Indian reservation located in the northeastern section of Washington State, within an area generically known as the Columbia Plateau. The actual reservation encompassed lands that "extended from the Columbia River in the east to the Okanagan River in the west and from the Columbia River on the south to the Canadian border on the North." Although somewhat diminished in size, the Colville Reservation remains in existence to this day. It includes among its confederated constituents six tribes: the Colville, Lakes, Methow, Nespelem, Okanogan, and San Poil. In 1927 they filed suit against the United States in the Court of Claims. Such a step was in fact the culmination of multiple efforts to gain access to it.

This court had been established in 1855, then strengthened and enlarged in 1863. Eighteen years later, in 1881, Congress enacted the first special jurisdictional act relating to an Indigenous tribe and authorized the court to "take jurisdiction of and try all questions of differences arising out of treaty stipulations with the Choctaw Nation, and to render judgment thereon." From that date until 1946, any tribe seeking redress for alleged grievances against the United States first had to obtain congressional enactment of an appropriate specific statute. The experience of the six tribes well indicates that such a course was not easy. Further, success at gaining access to the Court of Claims in no way guaranteed a satisfactory outcome before its judges. The efforts of the six tribes may be considered typical of a process that in fact was expensive, laborious, and time consuming.

In 1935, looking back on approximately fifty years since passage of the first specific jurisdictional bill for the Choctaw tribe in 1881, the assistant solicitor for the Department of the Interior, Rufus Poole, made a shocking statement to the congressional committee on Indian affairs. He admitted that the extensive number of claims "which still seek settlement . . . including those that come back to Congress after unsatisfactory treatment . . . cannot be estimated." But Poole assumed that "at the present rate of progress there would appear to be more than one century ahead of troublesome Indian claims." The process from getting a bill introduced into Congress to filing a suit before the court took an average of about eight years. Moreover, the tribes were "persistent plaintiffs and they return session after session, despite disregard, defeat, and veto, and regardless of whether they are meritorious or not." Poole specifically identified the Okanogan and Colville tribes who had already presented their claims to Congress half a dozen times.

The first step for a tribe, and one made more difficult by the distance of several thousand miles between the Colville Reservation and Washington, DC, was the selection of an attorney, one who presumably possessed several specific attributes: (1) familiarity with past treaties between the various tribes and the United States; (2) some rapport (understanding) with the tribal leadership; (3) intimate knowledge of the legal bases (statutes and/or treaties) on which the tribes sought congressional authorization for their lawsuit; (4) personal acquaintance with a member or members of the congressional committees on Indian affairs; and (5) willingness to accept the attorney fees as set by the Department of the Interior, and sometimes actually incorporated into the statute under consideration. Apparently, William S. Lewis satisfied all these qualifications. A graduate of Stanford University and a member of the Washington State Bar since 1898, he informed the House Subcommittee on Indian Affairs in 1926, "I'm an attorney at law. I have been a resident of Spokane, Washington for more than forty years and maintain a law office there." Since 1924 he had represented the group of Indigenous Indians collectively known as the Colville and Okanogan tribes as they sought congressional passage of a special adjudicatory statute. Moreover, he was not only familiar with their claims but also appeared before this subcommittee "with the approval of the Indian Office and the Interior Department." In this respect, Interior Secretary Hubert Work had informed the House panel that these two tribes "were recently allowed to employ an attorney . . . as they felt that they had certain claims on account of a large area of land they once occupied" in the state of Washington. An earlier attempt to gain the special act had come in 1925. Because it differed in a key essential from later bills, the 1925 version deserves some discussion.

In terms of content, the special acts varied from Congress to Congress depending on the makeup and preferences of the committees involved. At the outset, therefore, political concerns intruded into what should have been solely a judicial question. Matters as mundane as the reputation in Congress of the bill's sponsor(s) as well as the attitude of the current administration could be important. Once the special bills reached the floor, however, they all shared, almost invariably, at least nine common characteristics:

(1) a statement of the authority to sue
(2) disregard of the statute of limitations
(3) a time limit for launching the suit
(4) advancement of the case on the docket
(5) access by plaintiffs to all relevant government records
(6) rights of the United States to plead set-off and counterclaims
(7) determination of attorney fees
(8) appeal to the Supreme Court
(9) some limitation on the "scope of the claims cognizable" by the Court of Claims

Assuming that a bill successfully satisfied all these conditions, of course there remained the sometimes insuperable challenge of gaining executive approval.

With one significant exception, H.R. 9160 adhered to these guidelines.

All claims of whatever nature, both legal and equitable, of the several Okanogan and Colville Tribes ... either growing out of any treaties or agreements made by such tribes or any of them, with the United States or growing out of the original Indian title of said tribes ... to lands and to hunting, fishing, and grazing rights alleged to have been taken away from said tribes ... by the United States, and all claims of whatever nature, both legal and equitable, which the several Okanogan and Colville ... or of any of them (with whom no treaty has been made), may have against the United States shall be submitted to the Court of Claims, with the right of appeal by either party to the Supreme Court . . . for determination; and jurisdiction is hereby conferred upon the Court of Claims to hear and determine any and all such claims and to render final judgment thereon.

Further, the tribes were given up to five years after passage of this act to initiate suit, with the Okanogan as plaintiffs, and the United States as defendant. Finally, the Court of Claims was given authority to fix and determine a reasonable fee for the attorney employed by the tribe, "not to exceed 10% of the recovery, and in no event shall such fee amount in the aggregate . . . to more than $25,000 together with all necessary and proper expenses incurred in preparation and prosecution of the suit." With a unanimous report in favor, the subcommittee noted that "these Indians should have their day in court." The bill passed the House by voice vote and without any recorded debate. It received similar treatment from the Senate two days later. The exception referred to above reflects the fact that nowhere in the text of H.R. 9160 is there any reference at all to specific areas of land or territory for which compensation was sought. Whether intentional or not, perhaps this omission contributed to its ultimate fate—a pocket veto by Calvin Coolidge.

* * *

Barely a year later, on April 6, 1926, again Lewis appeared before the congressmen to explain, explore, and justify a proposed new and revised statute, one that included important specifics. The lands at issue, near or adjacent to the Colville Reservation, represented a not insignificant acreage, given the relatively small limits of the current reservation area. The claimed amounts for which the tribes sought compensation came to more than 450 million acres. At the standard 1926 federal price of $1.25 per acre, their value—according to Lewis—amounted to at least $5,672,680. To this sum, the tribes also added compensation for lost hunting, fishing, and grazing rights, which increased their claim by another $2 million. Thus the total claim for which the tribes sought congressional authorization came to more than $7,672,000.

Even before the congressmen heard from William Lewis, they had already received word from Interior Secretary Hubert Work that neither he nor President Coolidge supported the Colville and Okanogan Indians' latest request embodied in H.R. 9270, authorizing the tribes to make their case before the Court of Claims. Work cited three points. In the first place, while an earlier (1855) Blackfoot treaty mentioned "western Indians," Work claimed that the Indians now seeking congressional adjudicatory legislation were *not*—unlike other local tribes—specifically included in reference to the "common hunting grounds." Further, the same objection applied to the matter of fishing rights. Finally, Work insisted that not only had the Colville and Okanogan tribes been provided land on the Colville Reservation, but also they had "been furnished benefits by the Government, including gratuities." Indeed, he added, "it is believed that approximately 50 per cent of the amounts claimed would be offset by moneys appropriated, including gratuities, that have been paid to and used by these Indians." But even with the requested amount reduced by half, Work urged that the bill "not receive your favorable consideration," all the more as "the Director of the Budget has advised that that the proposed legislation in H.R. 9270 is in conflict with the financial program of the President."

Such a claim, perhaps containing a veiled threat of a veto recommendation to President Coolidge, did not faze the House Subcommittee on Indian Affairs. Examination of the *Congressional Record* from 1922 to 1934 reveals that a larger number of special bills permitting Indigenous tribes to seek relief from the Court of Claims appear to have been filed and enacted during this period than in earlier decades. Indeed, one historian describes the era as "a crusade for Indian Reform." Randolph Downes cited numerous quasi-muckraking articles revealing abuses within the Bureau of Indian Affairs and calling for federal intervention. Such publications were, in fact, nothing new. One possible explanation for their marked reappearance after 1922 may lie in the ongoing scandals of the Harding administration, particularly those involving Albert Fall, a former senator from Nevada and Harding's secretary of the interior from 1921 to 1923.

As secretary of the interior, management of the Indigenous tribes lay within Fall's jurisdiction. He resigned his cabinet post in March 1923 and appears to have been the first cabinet-level officer to be sentenced to prison for malfeasance in office. Further, the Indian Citizenship Act was introduced into the House on February 22, 1924, and passed that chamber in less than a month, with Senate approval coming on May 15. President Coolidge signed the bill into law on June 2. After this date, "all noncitizen Indians born within the territorial limits of the United States be, and they are hereby, declared to be citizens of the United States." With members of the Indigenous tribes now citizens, and supposedly possessing all the accoutrements that came with such status, one wonders why it was still considered necessary for them to gain a special act in order to bring a case to the Court of Claims. Be that as it may, congressional efforts for the Okanogan and Colville tribes to gain access to this tribunal had been much in evidence since February 1925.

Before William Lewis could begin his statement, Samuel Hill, a Democrat from the state of Washington, explained that his bill—H.R. 9270—had originally been introduced in an earlier version, but he "was advised that the Bureau of Indian Affairs thought it desirable that in these jurisdictional bills, the grounds upon which recovery would be sought should be set out; in other words, they should state specifically the grounds upon which the claims were based." Such was now the case with H.R. 9270. With these specific monetary figures and acreages set forth, Lewis launched into his presentation. It was based on one fact that distinguished his cause from other similar congressional proposals. By 1926 the vast majority of Indigenous tribes (and there were more than 450 of them) had made arrangements with the federal government that usually had resulted in claims to their lands being extinguished by treaty and acceptance of some sort of compensation to facilitate a move to a reservation. Repeatedly Lewis insisted that this pattern had not been followed with his clients. The "original, admitted, undisputed, and recognized Indian possessory rights of these tribes to a large expanse of country occupied and used by them has never been extinguished by treaty, agreement, or voluntary cession, . . . nor have [they] ever received any compensation therefore." To the contrary, the United States had simply "taken possession of their country," and the Indians "were pushed, crowded, and forced off from and deprived of the best of the lands they occupied [and] . . . of the hunting rights, fishing rights, root and berry appurtenances, and privileges enjoyed therewith and wherefrom they obtained their livelihood—all wholly without any compensation to them for the property taken from them." Such action, according to Lewis, violated Okanogan and Colville property rights long protected by the Fifth Amendment to the Constitution.

Moreover, these tribes had resided from time immemorial in

"peaceful, undisturbed, and long-standing possession of a considerable body of land" in what became the territory and later the State of Washington. Lewis cited newly appointed Supreme Court justice Harlan Stone, who, in his earlier capacity as attorney general, had stated in 1924 that "the Indian right of occupancy is as sacred as the fee title of the sovereign." Stone added that "the Indian title as against the United States was merely a title and right to the perpetual occupancy of the land, with the privilege of using it in such mode as they saw fit until such right of occupancy had been surrendered to the Government." Here Lewis reiterated his insistence that in fact the tribes had never surrendered anything. Perhaps the federal authorities had intended to negotiate some sort of treaty, but "various causes, the Indian War of 1855–1858 . . . the gold-mining excitement, 1855–1865, [and] the outbreak of the Civil War" negated such intent, "and no treaty or agreement was ever made with them."

Instead, "these Indians met a constantly increasing onrush of land-hungry settlers, intent on securing for themselves the best of the Indian lands, having no regard for the Indian or his rights, and actually seizing and dispossessing the Indians from enclosed fields and cultivated lands and improvements. The Indians were constantly and gradually forced off their best lands on to poorer lands the whites did not then want." The original Indian possessory right and title to the lands, for which claim is here made, has, however, admittedly never been ceded by these Indians nor relinquished to the United States. The matter was "neglected and overlooked." Lewis added that he had tried to get access "to the books of the General Accounting Office, but I was refused access to them. I am satisfied that these Indians have a big, substantial claim beyond any equities or offsets that the Government can show." Republican congressman Harold Knutson from Minnesota responded, "I rather think you have made a case." But Lewis had more comments for the subcommittee.

He urged the House subcommittee to reject the assertion in the federal commissioner's report that "these Indians are well off. The fact is that they have passed through six years of drought and probably one quarter of these Indians have gone on half rations in the past winter. They do not starve to death; but it debilitates them so that they merely exist, and they fall victims to diseases like pneumonia." Further, Lewis's clients "at all times . . . had held an original exclusive Indian possessory right and equity to all the lands embraced therein," from which they had been excluded and driven off." As to the territory onto which they had been forced, "the topography is rugged and very broken; high rocky hills and mountains, deep canyons, and gulches are the rule. Large areas are not suitable for any purpose."

Ultimately, these Indians have yet to be compensated

> for the loss of greater and more valuable tracts of land taken from them without their consent or for the abundant means of liveli-hood—fishing, hunting, root grounds ... of which they have been wrongfully deprived. There is practically no hunting left; the great salmon and other fisheries have been ruined ... and the lands where these Indians are allotted and now live are best suited for grazing purposes; and these Indians ... are in a situation ... where horses have been killed to leave food for cattle, and cattle sold to provide food for existence, and where many Indians have no money or means to purchase food, to say nothing of seed wheat and other agricultural necessities.

Lewis added that "the loss of the salmon and other fisheries was a most severe blow to these Indians; they still feel it. . . . It was the loss of half of their food supply for the family for the whole year."

Full examination of Lewis's testimony to the House Subcommittee on Indian Affairs indicates that the lawyer had more in mind than simply legal justification—based on multiple citations and quotations, all fully documented—for the jurisdictional statute he sought. In the final portion of his remarks, he turned to considerations that went well beyond the basic rules of law he had previously emphasized. He cited a letter dated February 4, 1926, received from a resident of the Colville Reservation, J. M. Lynch. After describing once again the unfortunate conditions facing the Colville Indians, Lynch observed,

> Conditions of this sort should not exist in this day of plenty. The wheels of justice move slow. The older Indians are going fast—struggle as patiently as it is possible, the load becomes too heavy and they fall by the wayside to be forgotten. Killed by the greed of the Christian white man in his cry of "make room for progress." ... I sometimes wonder if our Christian teaching is divine or just a smoke screen to hide the brute in the present generation of man.

For Lewis, the possessory rights he had urged on the subcommittee are "sacred rights." Not surprisingly, he cited the two famous holdings by Chief Justice John Marshall: the relation of the Indian nations to the United States resembles that "of ward and guardian," and the Indians are "wards of the government." (See *Cherokee Nation v. Georgia*, 30 U.S. 1 [1831], and *Worcester v. Georgia*, 31 U.S. 516 [1832].) To them, the United States owes "care and protection." Lewis noted a more recent decision (1877) that in dealing with the Indigenous tribes, "the United States would be governed by such considerations of justice as would control a Christian people in their treatment of an ignorant and dependent race."

In consideration of these claims, "and in granting these Indians the right at least to have the Court of Claims pass upon the merit thereof, Congress should bear these precepts in mind." This is not a situation that his clients "are in any way responsible for; what was theirs has been taken without their consent; without consideration to them; without any right or justice." Indeed, "civilized States though possessing plenary political power over their inhabitants do not confiscate the private property of dependent peoples, and to refuse to grant to these Indians the relief asked for would be contrary to and in violation of the Constitution." In short,

> every impulse and consideration of justice, of equity, and of fair dealing should prompt the Government at this late day not only in permitting but to assist and facilitate its Indian wards in the immediate, complete, and final presentation and proof of these claims which have become old and neglected through the sole fault and neglect of the Government itself in failing to initiate settlement . . . and in denying all opportunities to these Indians to prosecute these claims themselves before the Government's own tribunals.

Finally, Lewis reminded the subcommittee members of certain salient political realities. He informed them that the last Congress had enacted no fewer than twelve to fourteen similar laws, several of which involved claims totaling "many millions of dollars." Unless the tribes identified in this bill "are to be singled out and discriminated against they would appear entitled to the relief asked for in this bill." Further, while he did not do so, Lewis might have commented on the somewhat inconsistent course followed by President Coolidge in choosing whether to veto, pocket veto, or approve these measures. Although he approved a number of jurisdictional bills, he vetoed at least nine such enactments. Apparently no president who vetoed a special jurisdictional act regarding claims from an Indian tribe has ever had such action overridden. Counsel to the tribes added that "these long standing claims have been a source of irritation and deep-seated resentment against the Government . . . and from the standpoint of the progress of the Indians it would seem highly desirable that they be settled as soon as possible." Of greater importance is the fact that "many of the Indians most familiar with the facts on which these claims are based are getting old, and if their evidence is to be procured the right to sue must be granted, as without a jurisdictional bill the claimants are unable to preserve and perpetuate such testimony." Lewis concluded his remarks with a reference to the claim that the bill was opposed by the director of the budget, a point that had been raised earlier, even before he had started to speak. Courteously but candidly, he dismissed the point out of hand. It would not be "for some years to come," and it would be *only after* enactment of the bill that any obligation might confront the government. In the meantime any judgment that was rendered "shall be placed in the Treasury at 4 per cent per annum. The matter thus does not appear to present any financial consideration, concern, or embarrassment to the Government for a number of years to come."

* * *

The fact that the House subcommittee found William Lewis's testimony persuasive—even though it understood that such a special jurisdictional bill was only the beginning of what was an extended process, with ultimate success by no means assured—is demonstrated by the chronology involved. He spoke on April 6, 1926. Nine days later, on April 15, Harold Knutson submitted a report from the committee that H.R. 9270 "do pass without amendment." The explanatory portion of the report is barely two and a half pages in length, and at least 75 percent of it was taken verbatim from Lewis's earlier presentation, without—it might be noted—any acknowledgment. The report reiterated his key point that the government "has never extinguished . . . possessory Indian titles, except by express consent of the tribal bands expressed by formal treaty or agreement of relinquishment."

Whether through oversight or neglect, this step had never yet been taken. To be sure, in 1855 (as Lewis had also observed) Washington governor Isaac Stevens promised that "your rights are your rights and you shall not be deprived of them." It was his business, he had stated, "to protect you in your lands and rights." For more than thirty years, successive agents, commissioners, and government officials had "proposed, recommended, discussed, and negotiated . . . but nothing was done toward extinguishing this recognized outstanding Indian title." Moreover, these Indians had never made war on the whites. "They were simply crowded off their lands by pioneer settlers . . . backed by the coercion of government troops . . . and were tolerated only when they had been crowded onto a dry, wooded and mountainous section of the country that the whites did not then want, and whence it was physically impossible to force them to further pilgrimage." There, added Knutson, "they still wait for the justice and protection promised them by Stevens."

On the day following submission of its report by the House subcommittee to the full chamber, the Senate Committee on Indian Affairs held its own hearing on a bill identical to H.R. 9270. Once again William Lewis represented the group of Indigenous tribes. Even though the hearing was much shorter in length than the earlier House version, most of the key points had previously been mentioned. Lewis reemphasized that the "original possessory rights is [sic] admitted, the fact that the Government took this land, forced it from them, is also admitted; . . . and the only question . . . is whether there has been any agreement or settlement between these parties and the Government, and the record shows there has not." On being informed that the House subcommittee had unanimously reported out its bill the day before, Oklahoma senator J. Harreld suggested "that we adopt the hearings held before the House Committee. . . . I think that will simplify the matter because if we have further hearings here it will just duplicate what has already been done in the House."

*   *   *

On May 3 Montana Republican Scott Leavitt, chair of the House Subcommittee on Indian Affairs, sought to get quick approval for H.R. 9270, a not uncommon step for measures placed on the unanimous consent calendar. A non-lawyer, he would serve for five terms, before his defeat for reelection in 1932. But Leavitt ran into a roadblock in the form of Louis Cramton, Republican from Michigan, responding to the pro forma question "Is there objection to the present consideration of the bill?" Cramton observed that "we have of late been very freely sending to the Court of Claims a great number of omnibus Indian claim propositions." Furthermore, "these bill are being drawn in such wide open language . . . so that I believe the Congress ought to proceed hereafter with more care than they have in the recent past."

Leavitt and Sam Hill from Spokane were quick to respond that while Cramton could well be correct in reference to some previous proposals for adjudicatory claims, "the loose form is not being followed here." Indeed, H.R. 9270 had been drafted with the advice of the Bureau of Indian Affairs to deal with "a much more limited field in order to secure favorable consideration here in the House." Cramton was not deterred. He responded that the current claims that had been filed "aggregate a total of $408,000,000," to say nothing of a much greater amount for added interest. Over "a billion dollars is involved, [and] no one has any idea that if the rights of the Government are properly safeguarded[,] there is any considerable fraction of that amount due to the Indians."

Leavitt willingly conceded that while some attorneys had filed unreasonable claims, "it must be remembered that there are just claims still to be carried to the Court of Claims by different Indian tribes." Indeed, "this is a matter that has to do with the life and death of many old Indians. I have had Indians at the point of death ask me to get these things done before they died so that they will get the benefit. We must be fair and just." But Cramton remained unsympathetic.

He noted anew the firms of lawyers "who dig up these matters and present them and arouse in the Indians a feeling that they have got something coming to them." He continued,

If the Committee on Indian Affairs, the bureau, or Congress do not bow down to them and give them everything they ask for[,] they go out over the reservations reviling the administration of Indian affairs. As a result we are getting the Court of Claims and the Indian Bureau so clogged up with claims that have only a small percentage of basis in fact that the real claim, the real justice due the Indians cannot be secured.

To make matters worse as far as Cramton was concerned, this bill came in the face of negative recommendations from both the director of the budget and the secretary of the interior. He expected "to object to all these Indian claims on the Unanimous Consent Calendar," thereby delaying final House consideration.

This was enough for Leavitt. With an eye more on the future than the present, he sought "unanimous consent that [his] bill be passed over without prejudice." And so it was. It appears that not until June 23 did the House return to its Subcommittee on Indian Affairs. In the meantime, on June 3, by voice vote and without debate, the Senate quickly passed its version of the House bill, S. 3185. The House reconvened on June 23, a "Calendar Wednesday," by prior agreement with "the Committee on Indian Affairs having the call," which simply meant that any bills called up by it could be resolved by the full House acting as a committee of the whole House on the state of the Union. During the course of a session lasting more than a few hours, the chamber approved no fewer than seven bills called up by Leavitt on behalf of his committee, all by voice vote and without a roll call. While two such votes were taken concerning other matters than passage of the bills, it appears that Louis Cramton was not present for either of them. Although each bill was discussed separately, a number of congressmen offered comments related to all of them including the Okanogan-Colville proposal, the last of the seven to be voted on. For many in Congress these on-the-floor presentations by Leavitt and his colleagues provided important detail. Indeed, the background information on the Okanogan-Colville bill was more thorough than even the earlier hearings.

As debate got under way, Leavitt emphasized two key points: (1) that "nothing is or can be more important to the development of the Indians of the western country than the passing of these bills, allowing [them] to go into the Court of Claims and to have settled once and for all . . . whether or not they have certain amounts of money coming to them" from the US government, and (2) that the special adjudicatory acts to be voted on were not these "wide-open jurisdictional bills such as we passed in other Congresses and which have brought, I am sorry to say, a certain amount of criticism" on his committee. On the contrary, they identified the specific treaties and/or statutes under which actions may be brought. Possibly with President Coolidge's past pocket vetoes in mind, Leavitt added that "we felt it was unjust and unfair to the Indians . . . to report any bill out in a form we felt sure would meet with a presidential veto. We have tried to conform to the reasonable provision that treaties be specified and that a prima facie case up to a reasonable point shall be made."

Several congressmen observed that the amounts of interest to be paid the Indians varied from statute to statute, as did the total to be paid for legal representation. Leavitt explained that a limit of $25,000 "has barred certain tribes of Indians from securing the kind of legal talent that is necessary to give them a real representation in the courts." He continued, "Also we must take into consideration . . . that this is the form of a contingent fee, that the attorneys take these cases, meet their own expenses, go into the records, and that it is a matter sometimes of years. They take their chances on what they are going to get." On the other hand, a limitation of up to 10 percent of revenue recovered in a claim of $2 million represented $200,000. Carl Chinblom, a Republican from Chicago, added, "It occurs to me that in a case . . . involving $2,000,000 in claims, it is possible you will not be able to employ competent attorneys when you limit the fee to $25,000." Ultimately the House deleted the $25,000 limitation from the bill.

Leavitt faced a different kind of query from Illinois Republican Martin Madden. "I wondered," he observed, "whether the committee [on Indian affairs] "felt there was sufficient obligation imposed on the committee to write the report in such a way as to enable a Member who has not time to read the hearings, and many Members here have not, to understand the case and vote upon it intelligently." He was frank to say that "I have never seen a report on one of these bills I thought I could get an intelligent conclusion from as to what I ought to do, and so I have adopted the policy of voting against" them. It seemed to Madden that "we never have had, and we are entitled to have, a comprehensive statement of everything that is involved in the case when we are undertaking to pass legislation, and we have not that."

Leavitt replied that if the House desired a more complete report on these bills, his committee "would be very glad to comply with the request," but he added (possibly with Madden in mind) that as a general proposition, "the Indians being the wards of the Government and the statute of limitations having run, no Indian tribe can get its case before the Court of Claims without the passing of a jurisdictional act." Madden responded that "there ought not to be any undue haste . . . in loading the courts up with litigation on claims of doubtful propriety, as I consider many of these claims." In his comment, Madden might well have included those bills accompanied by an adverse recommendation from the Department of the Interior, as was the case with the Okanogan-Colville claim, to which the House would shortly turn. A colleague on Leavitt's committee, Harold Knutson, picked up on the point. A negative recommendation "does not mean that the claim is without merit. Are we to follow the sayso of someone down in the Department? If the tribes come before the committee and present a just case we will report out that bill for them."

Demonstrating persistence if nothing else, Madden asked members of the Subcommittee on Indian Affairs for some specific examples of treaty violations against a specific tribe, as well as an estimate of the value attached to hunting rights. William Williamson demurred. "I do not think it is the function of our subcommittee to enter into details to that extent. That is the function of the Court of Claims. It is for us to determine whether a right has been violated that ought to be adjusted. If we tried to ascertain the damage in every case, our job would be interminable." Madden remained unfazed. "The more time you spent, the less it would cost the Government and the more nearly perfect you would have your case." Furthermore, "I hope what I have said may have sufficient weight with the committee to induce it in the future to so prepare what they bring in here that there will be a pretty clear understanding from the report of what the proposed legislation means."

*   *   *

Scott Leavitt called up the last of the seven bills coming from the Subcommittee on Indians Affairs late in the lengthy session on June 23. After gaining quick and unanimous approval to substitute S. 3185 in place of the identical H.R. 9270, Leavitt turned the bill over to Washington State congressman Samuel Hill, who, it will be recalled, had played a major role in the earlier House hearing discussed above. He had also been the prime mover of H.R. 9160, which had passed Congress in 1925, only to receive a pocket veto from Coolidge. Hill began to explain this episode when Massachusetts Republican Charles Underhill asked if Hill would "go a little further and state whether he has any reason to believe that had there been more than sufficient time, the President would have signed the bill?" Hill replied, "I have no reason to believe it." Underhill added that "in fact, it has been intimated the President would have vetoed it if the time limit had not expired." Hill responded that "he might have vetoed it had the time required permitted such action. I am not endeavoring to present anything except the true situation."

Hill chose not to inform the House that in March 1925, after the pocket veto, he had written Coolidge that "as the record does not show the grounds of your objection to this measure I would greatly appreciate the favor if you will give me this information." Unaware of Hill's letter to Coolidge, Underhill asked, "There is no evidence in the report as to the reason which the President had for not signing the bill . . . ?" Hill replied, "No; nothing whatever, but to supply [Underhill] with that information, and in line with my purpose to make a frank statement," Hill read to the House the letter he had received in response to his request of the president. "My conclusions were based on the feeling that it did not seem fair to the Government at this time to undertake to litigate claims of such ancient origin. It seems to me that they rest under the general objection which justifies all statutes of limitation." Earlier in the month, Coolidge had pocket vetoed another special claims act, and in response to a letter from Congressman John Raker, had used the exact same language.

Hill further explained to his colleagues that the 1925 statute had been "a blanket form of bill," but in 1926 he had complied with the instruction from the Subcommittee on Indian Affairs that the particular grounds on which a claim was put forth were to be specified, as indeed they were in the bill before them. Hill may have hoped that this "fact would perhaps make some difference to the Executive in his . . . approving or disapproving the present bill, although [Coolidge] states in his letter that the claim is old and should be governed by the rules applying in cases coming within the statutes of limitation." He said no more about this subject, however, and instead turned to the history of the Colville-Okanogan claims. Possibly with Madden in mind, he provided in-depth background and detail for his listeners.

Hill began by reminding the House that the Okanogan-Colville claims were not based on treaties or statutes. These tribes had "occupied from time immemorial a section of country in the northeastern part of what is now the State of Washington." Even before the Hudson Bay operations, they were there, and so they remained undisturbed until the mid-nineteenth century. In 1855, fearing an outbreak of intertribal war, Isaac Stevens, the first territorial governor, proposed to negotiate treaties with a group of Indigenous tribes in the northwestern section of what would become Washington State. He did so with a number of treaties "fixing the boundaries of their lands, fixing their rights in the treaties."

Having dealt with tribes in the Northwestern territories, Stevens now planned to confer with the Northeastern tribes, among them the Colville and Okanogan, for the same purpose. Indeed, he called a council meeting in order to fix their "territorial boundaries and their rights growing out of their use and occupancy of the land which they had occupied from time immemorial." But Stevens suddenly was called away to deal with an uprising apparently at the hands of the Yakima tribe. Although both the Okanogan and Colville tribes were represented at this aborted meeting "ready to negotiate, anxious to negotiate, to settle their property rights," Stevens promised to return, and before leaving he had claimed that "your rights are your rights, and you shall not be deprived of them. . . . Now do not let your minds be troubled. I, your friend, say that your lands will not be taken from you."

However, as Hill conceded to his fellow congressmen, "there was never any further negotiation." Because the Okanogan and Colville "were peaceable and because they were not giving any trouble they were neglected; they were not treated with and their rights were never protected in accordance with the promises of Governor Stevens to them." They remained eager and even anxious to negotiate, "but one event followed after another," and no treaty as envisioned by him was forthcoming. The Yakima and Nez Perce Wars were followed by the discovery of gold, which was accompanied by a "great inrush of people into that country." Many of them settled on the lands of the Indians, where presumably they had no right to be. Perhaps the ultimate result in this litany of events was the failure of Stevens to return to the Washington Territory, as he was killed in the Civil War.

By executive order in 1872, President Grant established what Hill aptly described as "a curtailed Colville Indian Reservation," one that "embraced lands that were already included in the territory occupied by these Indians. It was simply a limitation of their territory rather than giving them something in exchange for something else." Ultimately, American military pressure forced their relocation to the northern part of the reservation, a mountainous territory "with deep valleys, rocky high peaks . . . but very little farming lands. . . . The incoming white settlers kept crowding them out of their lands [and] into this sterile, barren, cold, comfortless region that the white man did not then want." Such was their reward "because they have been the white man's friend. . . . If these Indians had been warlike and treacherous, they would have had their reservation and treaties would have been made which would have settled their property rights."

At this point a few congressmen asked some questions of Hill. "Are there," inquired Pennsylvania Republican Thomas Butler, "any lawyers engaged in these claims?" Hill acknowledged only one, but he did not disclose Lewis's name. He stated that the stipend for the lawyer would not exceed 10 percent and in no case to exceed $25,000. Butler probed further. "How long has he been working on it?" Hill replied, "Four or five years; and how much longer he will have to work before he gets the case ready for presentation to the Court of Claims I cannot say. It is a herculean task, for many of the old Indians have died, and it is more difficult as time goes on to get the evidence. That is one reason why the legislation should be passed as promptly as possible." As to the difference between this bill and the previous measure pocket vetoed by Coolidge, he added that the 1925 enactment had been a "blanket proposition which gave them the right to come into court and assert any claims that they might have or any that they might think that they had against the Government."

Lindley Hadley, a Republican from Washington state, clarified this distinction. "Is it not a fact that the prior bill did not express any limitations, whereas the present bill limits the demands within the particulars to which I refer—fishing rights . . . and hunting rights?" Hill immediately interjected, "And certain lands of which they have been deprived." In other words, responded Hadley, "there is express limitation in both those regards, which did not exist in the other bill, and the matter has never been before the President at all under the conditions stated in this bill." Although not raised by him, Hadley's underlying question was whether such a distinction would be of sufficient significance to warrant Coolidge's approval.

Hill further conceded that both the secretary of the interior and the Bureau of the Budget had been recorded in opposition to the bill. Representative Bertrand Snell, a Republican from New York, offered his answer to Hadley's unasked question. "As I understand, the provisions of this bill are such that they will meet the disapproving views of the President to the [earlier] bill when he had it before him and [pocket] vetoed it." Ultimately, Snell was prescient in his prediction. But for the moment, Hill concluded his remarks by emphasizing that "if there are any Indians in this country that are entitled to consideration by this Congress they are the Colville and affiliated tribes of Indians, and I submit to you that this bill should pass in order to do belated justice to these Indians. [Applause]." And so it did, without further debate, discussion, or even a roll call. William Lewis had his special act signed, sealed, and submitted to President Coolidge on June 24. At last the way was clear for his case on behalf of the Okanogan and Colville tribes to move forward. To be sure, the new statute only gave the tribes the right to present their claims to the court. But it was an auspicious beginning. Or so it seemed.

CHAPTER 3

Still Waiting at the Gates of the Court, 1926–1928

S. 3185 passed Congress on June 23, 1926, by voice vote, with neither a roll call nor any recorded evidence of opposition to its final passage. Signed by the appropriate congressional officers, the bill was formally presented to President Coolidge one day later. The president, however, did nothing concerning it. He did not sign the bill. He did not indicate acceptance or rejection of its contents to the legislature. He did not return it to either house of Congress, although that body did not adjourn until July 3. He did not deposit it with the secretary of state as a law. All during the summer of 1926, Coolidge appears to have made minimal mention of the bill, and when Congress reconvened for its second session on December 6, no return of the bill had taken place, nor had any specific objections to it been raised. It seemed clear, therefore, that S. 3185 had received a pocket veto from Coolidge. Seeking clarification of its status, on July 6 Washington State Republican Senator Wesley Jones twice contacted the president. First he telephoned the White House, and later that day he followed up with a letter. "I do hope," he wrote, that "you will feel justified in signing this measure." Jones could well appreciate the fact that "these claims may be old but the Indians will never feel satisfied until they have been adjudicated. If they have just and meritorious claims they are entitled to have them settled. If their claims are not just and meritorious I have no doubt that the Court will so find."

But Jones mentioned an additional reason for Coolidge to act positively concerning this bill.

I think the government can afford to deal rather leniently with these people who are its peculiar wards, and we can afford to act liberally rather than upon what may be technical principles in adjusting their claims. These Indians have really been good Indians [*sic*] and I think they deserve most liberal consideration on the part of the government. It will probably take three or four years to get their claim passed upon by the court.

Two days later, the president responded to Jones in a three-sentence letter. Coolidge offered no comments on the substance of S. 3185. "I have," he assured Jones, "given most earnest consideration to what you have said in support of this measure. However, I regret to say that I am very strongly inclined to the view that it should not be approved." The only way for Coolidge to implement this negative position, since Congress had adjourned, was to utilize the pocket veto. At this point a few words about this constitutional phenomenon may be appropriate.

The veto power is contained in Article I, Section 7, Clause 2 of the US Constitution. It mandates that every bill passed by Congress before it becomes a law shall be presented to the president. If Congress is in session, the chief executive has ten days (excluding Sundays) to act on it. He can either sign it or let it become law without his signature. If, on the other hand, he does not approve, he "shall return the measure to the House wherein it shall have originated together with his objections there to." If any bill has not been returned within ten days after it has been presented to him, it shall become a law whether he had signed it or not, "unless the Congress by their adjournment prevent its return, in which case it shall not become a law." These eighteen words are all there is to the pocket veto.

The origin of the term remains obscure, although the claim that it originated with Abraham Lincoln in 1864, when he refused to sign a Reconstruction measure and remarked to his secretary that he was putting it in his pocket, is probably apocryphal. However the name originated, our chief executives have clung to the practice with tenacity. Indeed, it has a venerable lineage in American presidential history. Only eight presidents never utilized the veto, and two of them—William Henry Harrison and James Garfield—had very short terms in office (a matter of months at most). The remaining five presidents who never employed either a regular or pocket veto included John Adams, Thomas Jefferson, John Quincy Adams, Zachary Taylor, and Millard Fillmore. Martin Van Buren appears to have used no regular vetoes, and a pocket veto only once in his entire term.

There are several distinctions between a regular and a pocket veto. In the first place, the traditional veto can be described as "a qualified negative veto." Along with the unsigned bill, the president may send a veto message, explaining his objections to the measure, sometimes indicating that a different bill with certain changes would receive a favorable reception when it reached the president's desk. Most important is the fact that when the chief executive returns the bill unsigned, Congress can override the veto by a two-thirds vote in each chamber. However, such a course, while possible, is not very probable. The first override, for example, did not take place until 1845, during the term of our tenth president, John Tyler. The relative rarity of a successful override can be seen in the fact that up to 2016, there had been some 1,508 regular vetoes, with only 111 overrides.

A second major distinction between the two is that the pocket veto is absolute. From such an act there is no appeal, no chance of an override, and little opportunity for any informed or sustained congressional debate concerning it, all the more so in that Congress is not in session at the time of the veto. Thus the potential presidential power inherent in a pocket veto should not be underestimated. It would appear to conflict with the famous (and traditional) conception of a tripartite structure of federal government with three equal branches. In a similar vein, the fact that the US Supreme Court has long arrogated to itself the power to declare an act of Congress unconstitutional brings into question how valid the conception of the equal branches of the federal government actually is. Further, the pocket veto has an air of finality to it, all the more so because presidents are not required—and since the mid-nineteenth century usually have not bothered—to provide any written explanation or specific justification for their pocket vetoes. Certainly this was true of Calvin Coolidge, who employed the pocket veto at least half a dozen times in disposing of special jurisdictional acts enacted by Congress for various indigenous tribes. To be sure, a pocket veto cannot be challenged by Congress, but a challenge to the supposed constitutionality of the practice itself represented a very different question.

Faced with the pocket veto of the second measure that he had drafted for the congressional committee on behalf of the Colville and Okanogan tribes, William Lewis undertook what seems to have been a rather unusual tactic: he wrote directly to President Coolidge. As a preliminary, on

October 18 he alerted Coolidge's secretary about the letter, writing that he "would deem it a great favor if you will bring my letter to his personal attention with the view of arranging an interview with the President for me." Lewis was aware that the secretary, Everett Saunders, would probably be the first to read Lewis's letter, and while he did indeed respond to Lewis, there appears to be no direct evidence that Coolidge himself actually read it. Also, this author was unable to ascertain whether or not Lewis ultimately met with the president, but be that as it may, later on the same day he addressed a four-page missive to the chief executive.

At the outset Lewis reminded Coolidge that the Colville Indians "have certain unsettled claims against the Government, the existence of which has been recognized in the records of the Indian office for more than forty years." Further, their prima facie validity "has been established and recognized by . . . both House and Senate." Indeed, he added, "Congress has twice passed Indian jurisdictional bills covering these claims, but bills have not been enacted into law through failure to secure Executive approval." Now, as Lewis was preparing for a new and third bill, "tentative objections" raised against the granting of such relief seem "to me, on careful consideration, not to be of such a nature as should prevent these neglected Indians from securing the relief asked for."

Although he might have considered it unnecessary, nevertheless the lawyer emphasized anew that the two earlier attempts and his forthcoming draft "[do] not ask for anything but the granting of the bare right to these Indians of submitting whatever claims they may have to the Court of Claims for adjudication, the prima facie merit of which has [previously] been established." This fact "has always seemed to me sufficient in itself to warrant and assure . . . the bare right to have the courts adjudicate them." Lewis acknowledged, however, that not all—including the recipient of this letter—agreed with him. Therefore he turned to several points that had been proposed as to "why these Indians should not have their day in court."

In the first place, it had been suggested that "the claims are old." Again, although he did not do so, Lewis could have observed that Coolidge himself had twice used the term "ancient claims" to describe them, and he would employ it again. But the attorney readily conceded the point. "This is obvious, but the Indians never having yet been granted the right to prosecute these claims against their guardian (the government,) the whole fault of their staleness falls to the government, and is neither attributable to these Indians nor a bar to their right. If anything this long delay in settlement should be an added reason for their prompt consideration now." In effect Lewis demurred to the point that the claims were too old. A demurrer can concede the validity of the point at issue, even while insisting that there is not sufficient justification to proceed with the case. The demurrer would be pivotal to the outcome of this study, although Lewis probably was not yet aware of this possibility in October 1926.

Counsel for the tribes further conceded that the government was temporarily "embarrassed by [so] many similar claims" having been authorized by Congress. Yet the legislature had "met this objection in the last deficiency appropriation bill" with an appropriation of more than $1 million "to cover the cost of [an] additional clerical force to examine records in connection with these jurisdictional bills, and therefore in effect negated this objection." Of possibly greater importance to Lewis was an assertion that had previously been raised during congressional debate over both the Colville and Okanogan bills, that they "are contrary to the financial policies of the Coolidge Administration."

Indirectly, the lawyer reminded Coolidge of two facts concerning the congressional session just concluded. During its term, the legislature had passed a number of special jurisdictional acts, as has been seen. While Coolidge had vetoed several of them either by regular or pocket veto, he had also signed others into law. As Coolidge was known for his legendary taciturnity, even though it appears to have been more calculated than natural, the few regular vetoes that he sent to Congress concerning tribal jurisdictional acts were short if not cryptic. He rarely offered any explanation for his pocket vetoes. Indeed, "an analysis of the legislative record of the last session shows that other Indian jurisdictional bills of an identical character with the Colville Jurisdictional Bill were enacted into law not withstanding this objection."

As to Lewis's implied criticism of alleged inconsistency, the president seems to have ignored it. In addition, Lewis queried how these jurisdictional bills were actually contrary to the administration's financial policy. As they relate not "to the incurring of new obligations but to the settlement of long outstanding claims, [and] involved no immediate payment of money [but] merely refer a settlement to the Court of Claims where it will obviously be years before a record can be made and a decision announced; no additional or immediate financial obligation is imposed on the government thereby, and these objections would therefore, seem on such analysis, inapplicable."

Assuming for the sake of argument that the tribes did win in the Court of Claims, in a somewhat convoluted sentence, Lewis presented a likely scenario to the president.

Even if payment was contemplated the maximum amount of the claims here consists of but a few million dollars, and the court recovery thereon in all probability will be far less than the maximum amount of the claim, and the total so small in contemplation with the aggregate expenditures of the government as to afford no grounds for embarrassment or objection from the standpoint of their financial consideration and ultimate payment.

In truth, Lewis added, "it is not a new obligation but one which in equity would have been discharged a generation ago."

Not until the bottom of his third page did Lewis finally get to the essence of his issue with the president. He wrote,

I have been unable to understand why the Executive Department has been, and is, so strongly inclined to the view that these jurisdictional bills (conferring on these Indians the bare naked right to have their claims adjudicated by the Court of Claims) should not be approved. I would, therefore, appreciate a statement from the Executive Department of the exact specific objection moving it in barring these Indians from the right to go to court.

Moreover, "if these claims in the final analysis have little or no merit, the court would appear to be the established and most satisfactory tribunal to decide that question, and why should it not be submitted to them?" This author could find no evidence that Coolidge directly responded to Lewis. His secretary acknowledged receipt of the letter, however, and informed the lawyer that he should take up the matter with the secretary of the interior, "to whom he referred it."

* * *

In response to the pocket veto that occurred sometime after Congress had adjourned *sine die* on July 3, 1926, legislative leaders had very few options. An override of a pocket veto was impossible. Nothing, how-ever, prevented Congress from passing the bill again, leaving—hope-fully—some time for "negotiations" between Congress, the Bureau of Indian Affairs, the Department of the Interior, and of course President Coolidge. Indeed, the House convened for its second session on December 6. Within three days, a new bill had been introduced, referred to the Subcommittee on Indian Affairs, and reported out to the full House by Harold Knutson. Careful examination of H.R. 13492 appears to indicate that the only thing new about the measure was its number. What Knutson reported out in fact was the old bill H.R. 9270, which had been passed as S. 3185 and had just been pocket vetoed.

The narrative of the report was virtually unchanged. It reiterated the comments first made by William Lewis and later "appropriated" by the committee for its report. Knutson further included the original unfavor-able recommendation by Interior Secretary Hubert Work and did not even bother to change the number from the old one, H.R. 9270. As it had done once before, the committee again reported the bill without amend-ment and recommended that it "do pass." Committed to the Committee of the Whole House on the State of the Union, the bill was placed on the unanimous consent calendar for January 3, 1927.

On being called up, and in response to the question "Is there objection to the bill?" the same roadblock in the form of Michigan representative Louis Cramton reappeared once again. "This is a bill," he stated, "that is disapproved by the [Interior] department and also by the [Bureau of the] Budget. More than that, it would authorize submitting the claims of another band of Indians, and already we have passed enough bills to keep busy for five years as large a force of auditors and employees as can get access to the books. Therefore I am obliged to object." Possibly trying to keep the bill on track, the Speaker insisted that "this bill requires three objections." Immediately, however, two more members objected, leaving the Speaker no choice. "Three objections have been made and the bill will be stricken from the calendar." And so it was. This author could find no evidence that this specific bill was taken up again by the House.

The proclivity to repackage the same bill in a new number for a new session was not limited to the House. In February 1927 the Senate did exactly the same thing with the same bill. On February 3, the Senate Committee on Indian Affairs reported out S. 4611. The report observed that "this bill is identical with S 3185, 69th Congress, 1st session, which passed both Houses of Congress and was presented to the President, but did not receive his approval before the adjournment of Congress." The Senate report also included a new letter from the Interior Department urging that S. 4611 not be enacted, as it "is in conflict with the financial program of the President." Four days later, without debate, discussion, or a roll call, the Senate passed S. 4611. In the absence of *any* specific comment from the Senate concerning S. 4611, speculation offered as to what the upper chamber intended by its action would be of limited value. While the House apparently failed to reenact its own identical measure, in 1928 the Senate again would pass a bill virtually identical to S. 4611. In the meantime, the lawmakers dealt with yet another special jurisdiction statute. On this occasion, discussion did indeed take place, and by examining some rather spirited debate in the House between members who by now will be familiar to the reader, some possible insights into congressional motivation may become clear.

Early in January 1927 the House turned to consideration of a Senate bill authorizing the Shoshone tribe of Indians to submit claims to the Court of Claims against the United States. William Williamson, representative from South Dakota and chair of the Subcommittee of Indian Affairs charged with consideration of special bills authorizing submission of claims, spoke on behalf of his subcommittee. Williamson had been a circuit judge for ten years in South Dakota before his election to Congress in 1921. He served from 1921 to 1933 and was defeated for reelection in the Democratic sweep of 1932. In his report recommending House approval for the Senate measure, Williamson had described it as "one of unusual merit." Unlike the Colville and Okanogan tribes, the Shoshone had signed not one but two separate treaties with the United States. In the 1868 Fort Bridger Treaty, the United States agreed that the current reservation "shall be and the same is set apart for the absolute and undisturbed use and occupation of the Shoshone Indians," and further "solemnly agrees that no persons except those herein designated . . . shall ever be permitted to pass over, settle upon, or reside in the territory."

Notwithstanding these specific agreements and in blatant violation of them, added Williamson, in 1877 the United States had resettled the Arapahoe tribe on half of the Shoshone reservation by military escort "for a year, or at most two years." Half a century later, the Arapahoe were still there, in spite of repeated complaints by the Shoshone, who "up to this good day have been refused any relief." Indeed, "even the poor privilege of going into court has been denied them." Further, "whatever may be the right of Congress to modify or abrogate a treaty with Indians, it is certain that the President or other executive officers of the Government have no such right, except [when] the Indians legally consent thereto." Therefore, "the action of [the Government] in placing the Arapahoes upon the Shoshone reservation and leaving them there to usurp permanently one half of it was clearly illegal. Congress at no time has sanctioned such action and the Shoshones have never consented thereto." Williamson rejected out of hand the contention that since the government had acted in good faith, "it should not be held responsible for any damage that might be suffered by any of its wards on account of its acts." He insisted that the good faith doctrine cannot be applied when there has been a violation of treaty rights, as was the case here. He developed his argument by citing the Northwest Ordinance of 1787, which provided for the Indians that "their lands and property shall never be taken from them without their consent; and in their property, rights, and liberty they never shall be invaded and disturbed. . . ." unless in just and lawful wars authorized by Congress." He also quoted from a Supreme Court case stating that "the purposes of the treaty could not be defeated by the action of executive officers of the Government."

Williamson further detailed previous efforts to get relief for the Shoshone through Congress. The Shoshone reservation as set aside in the 1868 treaty contained about 1,520,000 acres, of which one-half or 760,000 acres "had been turned over to the Arapahoes in violation of treaty obligations." The measure Williamson reported out "allows recovery for the value of the land as of the day taken, and 5 percent interest on the recovery from such date." Little complication "in making distribution of recovery is anticipated," he added, as "the two tribes have not mixed to any considerable extent." There seemed no doubt that the Shoshone property "has been taken from them without due process of law," with no compensation given or offered. Of course, after half a century, it would be both impractical and impracticable to have the Arapahoe evicted. But the Shoshone "do ask for an opportunity to seek a recovery for their losses in the Court of Claims." Williamson insisted that "in all fairness this should be granted." It seemed to the former judge that "out of all the bills our subcommittee has considered, this bill has as much or perhaps more merit than any of them. I am one of those," he remarked to the House, "who believe that these old Indian claims ought to be settled and gotten out of the way, and that the sooner they are tried and submitted . . . the better it will be not only for the Indians but for the Government of the United States."

Williamson had spoken without interruption, but when he asked unanimous consent to extend his remarks in the *Record*, Michigan Republican Louis Cramton intervened. "So far as I know anything about this claim," he began, "I think it is not as bad as some that the Indian Affairs Committee has reported to the House." For Cramton, however, the issue was not so much quality as quantity. "The trouble is that the Committee on Indian Affairs" not only under Leavitt's leadership but also that of his predecessor "has been sending to this House such a great grist of these bills that the hopper is all clogged up, and when a good case comes along, even if we were to pass the jurisdictional bill, relief could not be secured . . . because in the last Congress we passed so many of these jurisdictional bills" that if we give [the executive departments] "the money to hire as large a force of auditors and experts as could use the books of the Indian Department at one time, they would be five years in presenting the information the Government is obliged to furnish under these bills."

To make matters worse, "since then, in the last House we passed several more." Cramton continued,

> I have a very high regard for the Committee on Indian Affairs, and for its membership. but it seems to me that there is too much of the policy in that committee of "you report out what I want and I will report out what you want," with the result that every jurisdictional bill comes out of that committee. While the bill before us is better than some of the others, yet the machinery is clogged up for five years. . . . I think that so long as that committee reports out about all the bills sent to it of this character, somebody ought to have like consistency and object to them all.

Although later Leavitt had nothing but kind words for Cramton, on this occasion his irritation with his colleague was palpable. In effect Cramton was criticizing Leavitt's committee "for doing its duty and considering the measures that are placed before it." Cramton himself was chairman of an appropriations subcommittee "handling one bill a year, and because that bill contains items that have to do with appropriations for Indians," apparently he "feels that makes him an authority on the Indian question, and therefore he is in a better position to say whether or not a bill should be presented to this Congress" by other than Leavitt's committee. It did not, "as has been intimated by [Cramton,] pass them because somebody has asked for them. I think that is an intimation that is below the dignity and position of [Cramton] in this house and that he should not state such a thing on the floor of the House."

While Cramton failed to apologize for his remarks, in what can be described as an "afterword" he indicated that he might have had in mind the recent rush to attempt to repass legislation concerning the Colville and Okanogan tribes, discussed above. He stated,

> Having such high regard for the gentleman from Montana [Leavitt] and the other gentlemen on that committee, I was at a loss to understand in any other way how this thing happened. When I see a bill vetoed once by the President . . . and then, again disapproved by the department and disapproved by the Budget, and therefore disapproved by the President, sent out by this committee, disregarding all that former action, I think there must be some explanation behind it.

Leavitt responded that his committee "has not learned this job of back scratching. It believes that we should make an attempt even if it takes five years for the Government to catch up on these bills allowing these Indians to take their cases into the Court of Claims like other citizens of this country. They have been pounding on the doors of this Congress for 50 or 75 years to get an opportunity." Harold Knutson asked, "Why not abolish Congress if we are going to follow the absolute policy of the Director of the Budget and some of these bureaus?" With Knutson's query, the House moved on to other matters.

It did not return to the Shoshone issue until January 17, when S. 2301 was called up again. This time New York representative Fiorello La Guardia, for whom the future held election as mayor of New York City, objected. He stated that the bill "is not approved by the Secretary of the Interior and is in conflict with the President's budget program." Thomas Blanton also objected, but no other representative joined them, and three were required to block consideration. Thereafter by voice vote, with no recorded discussion or debate, and with the addition of a minor amendment, the bill passed. The Senate concurred with the change, and the bill was submitted to President Coolidge, who vetoed it on January 28.

A key provision of the law provided that if the Court of Claims found the Government in violation of any law, treaty or agreement, "damages therefor [*sic*] shall be confined to the value of the money, lands, or other property at the time of such appropriation or disposal, together with interest thereon at 5 per cent per annum from the date thereof." Although Coolidge implied that by accepting moneys based on agreements signed in 1896 and 1904 the Shoshone had acquiesced in the division of their reservation, Coolidge added that "still, this objection might not be fatal." Rather, it was the provision for interest that made the bill objectionable. "It seems to me unreasonable," he wrote, "to expect that the Government should be charged with interest from the dates of origin of such ancient claims. The amount of the interest . . . is several times greater than the amount of the principal."

Here Coolidge, perhaps recalling his days as an attorney in practice, drew on an argument very familiar to the legal profession, the slippery slope contention. This interest policy "would inevitably mean that issues supposed to have been placed in the way of fair determination by jurisdictional acts of the past will come forward again for additional interest settlements far exceeding the amounts of the original claims." Here Coolidge added a sort of quasi-offer to Congress. "Should the item of interest be eliminated, I can now see no reason why the bill should not be approved." But "if interest is allowed on this claim, it will certainly result in an effort to reopen an endless number of claims which have already been settled." No evidence has been located that indicates either any congressional challenge to this veto or efforts to enact a different version during the remainder of Coolidge's term.

In the spring of 1928 Congress passed another special adjudication act, this one on behalf of a group of tribes located in Washington State, adjacent to the Colville-Okanogan Reservation. The bill received passage in the Senate on April 24 and the House on May 7. As with other such measures, in each chamber there was no recorded debate, discussion, or roll call on S. 1480. It was approved by voice vote, and indeed, minimal time appears to have been devoted to its passage. After the bill was promptly presented to Coolidge, the president returned it to the Senate with a veto message on May 18.

Coolidge's language brings to mind the president's earlier letters to Congressmen Hill and Raker concerning his pocket vetoes of the Colville-Okanogan statutes. He concluded that "these claims are not based upon any treaty or agreement between the United States and these Indians, nor does it appear to me that they are predicated upon such other grounds as should obligate the Government at this late date to defend a suit of this character." The president reiterated his insistence that "the Government should not be required to adjudicate these claims of ancient origin unless there be such evidence of unmistakable merit in the claims as would create an obligation on the part of the Government to admit them to adjudication. It seems to me that such evidence is lacking." One day later, Coolidge issued yet another veto message. This one concerned a special claims adjudication act on behalf of the Cowlitz tribe. Coolidge merely quoted his earlier veto just mentioned, adding that "the same objections apply to this bill."

Between 1924 and early 1929, Calvin Coolidge vetoed fifty bills submitted to him by Congress. More than half of them were pocket vetoes. Of the twenty regular vetoes, the legislators overrode only four. None of them concerned a special adjudicatory bill for an Indigenous tribe. The great majority of his vetoes dealing with the tribes took the form of pocket vetoes accompanied by neither any explanation nor justification. Key among them, of course, were the two dealing with the Colville and Okanogan tribes. By early 1927 it probably was clear to William Lewis that the most feasible course for his clients would be passage of another special bill that would meet Coolidge's concerns. But as this chapter has demonstrated, such a bill, while it might pass one house, would not get through the other. Well aware that more than seven months (far beyond ten working days) had elapsed since June 24, 1926, when the special act was submitted to the president, on March 26, 1927, he filed a petition in the Court of Claims as authorized (or so he thought) by the statute.

PART II

The Pocket Veto:
Challengers and Challenges

CHAPTER 4

Reacting to the Pocket Veto, 1927–1928

During the second session of the Sixty-Ninth Congress, some legislators had attempted to enact another special jurisdiction statute for the Colville and Okanogan tribes. Early in 1927, as William Lewis awaited the outcome of this unsuccessful effort, members of the House engaged in a debate that centered on a different bill, H.R. 5218, which also had received a pocket veto from Calvin Coolidge, titled "An Act to carry into effect a certain provision of a treaty between the Shawnee Tribe and the United States proclaimed in 1868." On February 26, 1927, Oklahoma representative Charles Carter moved to amend a deficiency statute that was up for debate. He sought to add the sum of $463,732 to be expended in accordance with H.R. 5218, the bill that had been sent to Coolidge on July 3, 1926. Immediately, Indiana Republican William Wood raised a point of order on the grounds that "there is no authorization of law for this appropriation" because of Coolidge's pocket veto. The ensuing debate and its outcome offered a possible future course of action to Lewis, one he ultimately pursued.

Carter stated that the bill had been submitted to Coolidge on July 3 but "never received his action, either favorable or unfavorable." This "law" had not been "recorded as [a] statute." Thereafter a resolution had been introduced into the legislature declaring the bill to be a valid act of Congress because "it had passed both Houses . . . had been submitted to the President, and had not been vetoed by him within the 10 day limit required by the Constitution." Referred to a subcommittee of the Committee on the Judiciary, this group unanimously concluded that regardless of Coolidge's inaction, H.R. 5218 had indeed become a law. The full Judiciary Committee concurred and had reported the measure out to the full House, where it lay pending as Carter presented his amendment.

Congressman Wood responded that the subcommittee had failed to include in this proposed resolution (the subject of Carter's amendment) an appropriation for more than $400,000 because "there had been no recommendation coming to the committee from the Budget [Committee]." Such an omission led Wood to raise his point of order that there was in fact no authorization in law for Carter's motion. Carter replied that the real question is "whether or not the Shawnee claims bill has become a law by limitation." Of this the Oklahoma congressman had no doubt. He stated,

> The point is that the President did not return the bill within the time required by law, and that the adjournment on July 3 . . . did not constitute a legal adjournment of the Sixty-ninth Congress, as it had only adjourned until the first Monday in December. . . . All bills, resolutions, and other measures introduced in that session of Congress were just as alive in this session as they were before this temporary adjournment.

Carter insisted on repeating his point for emphasis. The Congress had not closed on July 3. "That was only the closing of [its] first session." Thus the contention by the subcommittee that the Shawnee bill had indeed become an act of Congress by limitation "is well taken."

The chairman of the House Committee on the Judiciary, Pennsylvania Republican George Graham, agreed with his conclusion. "This bill became a law and is a sufficient ground for overruling the point of order." Charles Christopherson, a Republican from South Dakota, offered further support for Carter's viewpoint. "The adjournment of July 3 . . . was not a final adjournment. The Sixty-ninth Congress was still in existence; the Speaker of the House was still Speaker; the Clerk was still Clerk; the entire organization of the House retained its place. It was the same identical Congress that reconvened in December." Christopherson's strong endorsement is understandable as he was the chair of the subcommittee whose unanimous report urged that H.R. 5218 be considered a law.

William Wood offered an observation "with reference to the precedent that may be established by reason of the Chair's ruling, and I do it for the purpose of assisting the Chair in his decision, whatever that may be, on the question whether or not this Congress is bound by a decision that comes from the Committee on the Judiciary." Wood had raised the point of order currently under debate. Now he stated further, "In my judgment, the opinion that has been inserted in this report is entirely extrajudicial. It cannot bind anybody, and it is of no more force and effect than if the same opinion came from some other committee of the House." Wood added, "I say this with all due respect and deference to the [judiciary] committee," which had cited various authorities in support of its decision, but "while the opinion . . . may be illuminating . . . it should not be binding for the reason that this has been a most extraordinary proceeding." Moreover, "the Chair can not take judicial notice of a bill that is not a law." He must take "judicial notice of the law that is published as a law. This bill has never been so published or declared." In other words, did the president possess the constitutional authority to "pocket veto a bill during the recess between sessions of the same Congress"?

No congressman appears to have been more supportive of Christopherson and Carter than another member of the Committee on the Judiciary, Hatton Sumners, a Democrat from Texas. Described by Jeff Shesol as "sour-faced [and] tart-tongued," ultimately Sumners would serve in Congress for thirty-four years, including a sixteen-year term as chair of this committee from 1931 to 1947. In addition to his negative comments on Wood's point of order, in another forum the Texas congressman would have much more to contribute on the subject of the pocket veto. For now, he spoke at some length to his colleagues, trying to explain why the point of order issue was inappropriate, incorrect, and unnecessary. He reiterated several points that had been made by previous speakers but took a different approach to Coolidge's course of action.

Sumners began with a lucid explanation of congressional authority as set forth in the Constitution. He then moved to the key question, whether or not by adjourning on July 3, 1926, Congress had prevented Coolidge "from having the time specified in the Constitution in which to examine H.R. 5218, formulate his objections thereto, if any, and return the bill, together with his objections to the House."

Next Sumners turned to the nature of the congressional adjournment. "When we adjourned on July 3," he stated, "we did not terminate the Congress. We did not in fact adjourn sine die . . . We recessed. We call that a sine die adjournment, but it was not an adjournment without day." In accordance with the Constitution, Congress had adjourned to the first Tuesday in December, and when the representatives gathered again on that day, "we reconvened not as a different Congress from that . . . which

[had] adjourned" but "we reconvened the same Congress, to continue as though there had been no interruption, no break in point of time. Bills were not reintroduced, committees did not begin their work de novo." Indeed, the work of Congress began "exactly at the point at which we stopped at the end of the last session ... no going back and beginning over." In truth, insisted Sumners, "the effect of the adjournment on last July upon legislation then pending and upon every legislative process, was the same, no more and no less, as will be the effect of the adjournment this evening at the end of this day's session." In other words, "that adjournment in July clearly did not prevent the President from having the 10 days specified in the Constitution to examine [the bill] and return the same to this House with his objections, if he had desired to do so."

Wood refused to give up. "I have this observation to which I desire to call the attention of the Chair before he rules, and that is the appropriation asked for here is not based upon law, but it is based upon a bill. That is not a law.... Whatever opinion the Judiciary Committee may have rendered is of no more avail, force, and effect than if it had been rendered by the Agricultural Department." The chair of the House Committee on the Judiciary sought and succeeded in having the last word. The presiding officer, as well as the entire House, knew "from the history of this legislation that it went into the President's hands, that the Congress did not adjourn finally and that it has never been returned to the Congress. These are the facts."

At that point the chair announced that he was ready to rule. He stated that the "question presented by the point of order is somewhat doubtful and has been the subject of much discussion." With some prescience he added that "it probably never will be definitely and finally settled until a decision is rendered by the Supreme Court." He conceded that the bill had passed both houses, and that "there is a legal presumption that the appropriate congressional officers had performed their duty," and that the bill "reached the President's hands." To be sure, "the resolution reported by the Judiciary is merely the opinion of that committee." Nevertheless, "it is an opinion rendered by attorneys of the highest standing and reputation," who "had all the time necessary and rendered a unanimous opinion that the statute in question had been legally enacted." Such an opinion, "therefore, although not binding on the House or binding on the Chair, is very persuasive at this time." Thus the chair overruled Wood's point of order, and with neither an appeal from this ruling nor any recorded vote, the House approved Carter's amendment.

* * *

Barely a month after the House colloquy concerning the legal status of H.R. 5218, William Lewis took the first step in implementing Senate bill 3185, discussed above in chapter 2. On March 28 he filed a petition in the Court of Claims. The petition of some fifty pages sought more than $13 million from the United States as compensation based on various grounds, and due to the six tribes mentioned at the outset of this study. Although Lewis had hinted at the gist of his complaint in his earlier testimony to the House Subcommittee on Indian Affairs, his statement represents the most detailed and expanded justification for their suit, and indicates that the attorney was prepared to make as strong a case as possible for his clients before the court.

In accordance with the 1862 statute that had expanded the court, Lewis affirmed—even though more than sixty years had passed since the end of the Civil War—that his clients "have not voluntarily aided, abetted, or given encouragement to rebellion against the defendant: and have at all times shown allegiance to the . . . United States; and that the petitioners believe the facts stated [herein] are true." Drawing on the arguments discussed above by Congressman Hatton Sumners, he noted of S. 3185 that it had passed both houses of Congress, had been duly submitted to the president, and "not being returned . . . within 10 days . . . now is a law in like manner as if he had signed it; the said 69th Congress . . . not having by its adjournment prevented its return." In effect, by committing himself to this line of argument, Lewis appears to have sought two interrelated goals: (1) to invite the Court of Claims to move into new legal territory concerning the constitutional provisions of the veto power, and (2) to sustain his clients in their quest for substantial monetary compensation.

Early in his petition, the attorney observed that these six tribes "have, from time immemorial and since the first records by white men lived adjacent to each other." Further, and "long prior to the advent of the first white explorers," they had "possessed, claimed and used as their own for fields, grazing, berry, root, fishing and hunting grounds" located within the "northeastern part of the present state of Washington."

Again, Lewis specified the locations of these various sites. After the 1846 Treaty of Washington in which the United States "acquired exclusive and recognized sovereignty over territories including what is now the State of Washington," the six tribes were "then in recognized, exclusive and undisputed possession of all the lands, rights and privileges." While the United States might now "own" the soil, the six tribes retained the exclusive possessory rights to the enjoyment and use of the soil and its appurtenances, within said limits, vested in and held by these tribes.

Lewis then cited no fewer than five separate provisions drawn from both statutory and case law that allegedly supported his clients' claims: (1) that these Indians "had the right and title to the perpetual occupancy of the lands . . . with the privilege of using it in such manner as they saw fit until such right of occupancy had been surrendered to the government"; (2) that such original possessory rights "would be extinguished only with the consent of the tribes recognized as having claim to the soil by reason of their occupancy thereof"; (3) "Nothing in this title shall be construed to impair the rights of any person or property pertaining to the Indians in any territory, so long as such rights remain unextinguished by treaty between the United States and such Indians"; (4) all of this territory "shall be excepted out of the boundaries, and constitute no part of any Territory . . . unless such tribe signifies its assent"; (5) the people of said states (Washington and Montana) "disclaim all rights to all lands lying within limits owned or held by any Indian or Indian tribes and that until the title thereto shall have been extinguished by the United States."

Close examination of these excerpts indicates two themes that link them together. In the first place, they all affirm the right of the tribes to retain possession of their lands even as they assume and anticipate action by the federal government to extinguish Indigenous title, presumably by agreement, treaty, and/or compensation. Further, they call for consent or assent on the part of the tribes to such action. Lewis built the second part of his petition around these two points. Indeed, to paraphrase an old popular American song, he argued that you can't have one without the other. The federal government could not seek to extinguish Indigenous land title unless and until they had gained tribal concurrence.

Lewis began the second part of his petition by pointing out that after ratification of the Treaty of Washington and the vast Washington Territory, his clients "became and ever since have been and now are wards of the defendant, and under [its] guardianship and control." Moreover, since the 1850s and to the present day, government officials have all been aware of the nature and extent of the areas including the hunting and fishing ground now in contention. In 1855 Superintendent of Indian Affairs—and later governor of Washington State—Isaac Stevens reached agreement with most of the tribes—"other than petitioners"—in Washington Territory. Stevens stated, "Your rights are your rights and you shall not be deprived of them. I, your friend, say to you that your lands will not be taken from you. It is my business as your friend to protect you in your lands and rights."

Before Stevens could conclude negotiations with representatives of the six tribes in 1855, he was called away by the outbreak of the Yakima War. Indeed, Stevens never returned to Washington. A number of incidents intervened, following in succession. They included Indian wars with "resulting disturbances and unrest"; "the gold mining excitements"; and delays in securing ratification of various treaties already negotiated, to say nothing of Stevens's death as a Union officer during the Civil War. All these factors combined to prevent the United States from concluding a treaty with Lewis's clients concerning "their recognized and unextinguished possessory rights and title." In the meantime, however, it had became increasingly difficult for the government to act because of other steps it had taken in the form of granting patents and conveying "to various private persons and corporations" title to the lands claimed and still possessed by the six tribes.

Using common contemporary language, Lewis insisted that until very recently, his clients "have been unused to white man's ways with respect to dealing with the . . . United States, and petitioners being poor and ignorant had no one, other than defendant's own agents, to represent and advise them." For years they had relied on the promises and assurances dating back to the mid-nineteenth century that the federal government "would protect petitioners in their said rights and lands." But such had not happened, and the realities facing them were quite different. The government had "invited white settlers to intrude upon petitioners' lands under the 'donation,' 'preemption,' 'timber culture,' 'homestead,' and similar acts, culminating of course in massive grants to the railroads—as though they were all part of the public domain," which, in fact, they were not.

It was in this context that the Colville Reservation had been established by executive order, even though Lewis repeatedly insisted that the tribes already possessed a better right and title than could be granted by the federal government. Furthermore, the boundaries of this reservation excluded the most arable and useful lands on which the tribes had lived for generations. While the six tribes sought to remain where they had been, inexorably they were "finally forced and driven from their lands." Three factors taken together contributed to this condition: (1) threats from the various Indian agents employed by the government; (2) active and implied coercion of military force displayed by the government; and (3) the "intrusions, threats and violence of white settlers invited into and upon petitioners' land . . . encouraged and protected by [the government] in a violation of all of petitioners' rights and privileges."

Lewis further emphasized that his clients "were and are a peaceful people" and "have never been at war with the defendant [the US government]." While they have indeed resisted "the steadily increasing encroachments of white settlers upon their lands and rights," it has been "in a patient, persistent and peaceful manner," even as "they were dispossessed of their homes, and fenced and cultivated fields, and threatened and assaulted, and . . . killed in disputes with white settlers in a peaceful effort to maintain their said title, rights and claims." It was no secret that the people in what became Washington State "desired petitioners' . . . lands and seized every pretext and opportunity to secure them and to procure the assistance of territorial and federal officials in forcing and compelling petitioners to remove from their good lands . . . to the barren lands of the Colville reservation." Finally, these Indigenous tribes "were crowded, forced and driven from, and deprived of all their ancient habitat, range, rights and privileges. . . . There was no other place to which defendant would permit petitioners to go or reside."

Their acquiescence in such a move should never be taken either as "an abandonment of their claims to lands and rights . . . or as acceptance of their [new] lands . . . as a consideration, satisfaction or release of any of their rights and claims." Such claims are what the tribes intended to pursue under S. 3185, now—presumably—a valid statute. But there was more. Having presented "the foregoing common recital of the origin and historical development of their . . . claims," in the final portion of his petition Lewis turned to each tribe's further legal grievances against the United States. Two examples may suffice. The Colville and Lake tribes claimed a loss of 1,238,144 acres. At the mandated sum of $1.25 per acre, the tribes sought an additional $1,547,680. The Okanogan and Methow tribes claimed a misappropriation by the federal authorities of 1,977,500 acres. At $1.25 per acre, they sought an additional $2,471,875. When the amounts of land "to which the [six tribes] were entitled and which had been taken from them for the use and benefit of the United States" were calculated, the sum for which William Lewis filed this suit was $13,048,039. Of course, actual recovery of these lands would be impossible, as settled non-Indigenous communities had long since become prevalent among them. However, tribes living on a reservation could do far worse than gain a $9 million legal settlement.

* * *

Lewis filed his petition in the Court of Claims on March 28, 1927, but the United States demonstrated no interest in confronting the specific points he had raised. About five weeks later, the Justice Department submitted a general traverse to Lewis's petition. The term simply meant a blanket denial of all the claims he had alleged. The next step, one far more important, came on June 28, when the department presented a motion to file a demurrer. In law, a demurrer is a legal variant of the question "So what?" A demurrer admits to no wrongdoing—in this case on the part of the United States—but assumes that even if true, the facts as detailed by Lewis were not sufficient and significant enough to warrant going any further. There existed no legal grounds for the case to continue.

If ultimately sustained, a demurrer effectively ends the case. In this instance such a finding would bar Lewis from arguing the merits of what he had presented with such care in his original petition. It would shift the focus of the case away from the Colville and Okanogan tribes and to a narrow legal issue of common law pleading. Indeed, it would render their claims irrelevant, thereby requiring no analysis, discussion, or ultimate findings by the court. Given the Coolidge pocket veto, from the perspective of the Justice Department, a demurrer might well have made good sense. It liberated the government attorneys from a heavy burden of detailed responses to Lewis's arguments.

Without comment, on July 6 the court granted the Justice Department's motion, and on the same day government attorneys filed the demurrer. For such an important matter, it was extremely short, exactly one sentence long. "Now comes the Assistant Attorney General and demurs to the petitioner in [this] cause for the reason that the same is not within the jurisdiction of the Court." This was so because the bill (S. 3185) allegedly had never become a law as a result of the pocket veto.

On January 9, 1928, the government filed its brief in support of the demurrer, a document barely nineteen pages in length. At the outset, the author noted Lewis's claim that by its action in June 1926, the Sixty-Ninth Congress had not finally adjourned, and that by his inaction, President Coolidge had permitted S. 3185 to become a law. The defendant asserted, to the contrary, "that the Congress by its adjournment did prevent the return of Senate Bill No. 3185; that the said bill did not become a law; that consequently the United States has not consented to be sued . . . and that the claim, not being founded upon a law of Congress, is not within the jurisdiction of the Court." There was no doubt that the bill was submitted to Coolidge on June 24 and that Congress adjourned on July 3, 1926. Nor was there any disagreement over the fact that this date was "several days before the expiration of the period provided by the Constitution for the Presidential consideration of the bill before returning it." With refreshing succinctness, counsel stated that the question before the court was simply "whether the retention by the President of bills presented to him less than ten days before the adjournment of the first session of Congress prevents their becoming laws." In other words, was the pocket veto constitutional?

There was, counsel conceded, "no decision by the Federal courts directly in point." He cited, however, a US Supreme Court decision handed down in 1899: *La Abra Silver Mining Co. v. U.S.* Justice John Marshall Harlan observed "but if by its action, after the presentation of a bill to the President during the time given him . . . for an examination of its provisions and for approving it by his signature, Congress puts it out of his power to return it, not approved, within that time to the House in which it originated, then the bill fails and does not become a law." He further noted an advisory opinion to President Benjamin Harrison received from his attorney general, William Miller, on December 28, 1892. Miller wrote, "Suppose Congress having met on the 1st of December were, on the 1st of February, to adjourn until the 1st of October. What would become of a bill presented to the President and not approved within ten days? It could hardly remain in a state of suspended animation until Congress should reconvene." Moreover, since Congress had adjourned, "the President could not veto it in the manner provided by the Constitution; and this being so, it would appear to follow that if not signed it must fail to become a law."

Miller cited an additional advisory opinion to the effect that in order for the president "to return a bill the Houses should be in session; and if by their own act they see fit to adjourn and deprive him of the opportunity to return the bill with his objections, and are not present themselves to receive and record these objections . . . the bill cannot become a law." Also, "there is no suggestion that he may return it to the Speaker or Clerk, or any officer of the House; but the return must be made to the House as an organized body." The author of this brief, Herman J. Galloway, claimed that examination of the Constitution's wording sustained the two advisory opinions just cited. The language providing for the pocket veto only mentions "adjournment" by itself. The framers failed to further distinguish the term. "If the framers . . . had intended that the provision should apply only to an adjournment by Congress at the end of the term for which it was elected, they would have expressed that thought more definitely." Taking the text as written, "they clearly intended the provision to apply also to other adjournments, as at the end of a session. They also thought that such an adjournment would prevent the return of a bill of which the President disapproved," as was the case here.

Galloway insisted that President James Madison "clearly understood that he could not return a bill to Congress when that body was not in session." More than any president before him, "he had had abundant legislative experience in Congress [both] under the Articles of Confederation and . . . under the Constitution. He could act with authority on this point. And his interpretation of the Constitution is entitled to great weight, for he had taken a more important part in its framing than any other member of the Convention of 1787[,] and he understood its basic principles most thoroughly." For the remainder of his brief, Galloway simply cited various examples of other presidents who had seen fit to retain various congressional measures after the legislature had adjourned. He concluded by another reference to the La Abra Silver Mining case, 175 US 423 (1899), with which his brief had started. Now he repeated once again that if by its action [adjournment] "Congress puts it out of his power to return it, not approved . . . then the bills fails and does not become a law. This, defendant submits to the Court is precisely what Congress has done in the present case."

It remains unclear whether or not Lewis had anticipated such a formidable legal roadblock in the motion for a demurrer. There is no doubt that he realized the seriousness of such a move. In response to Galloway's brief, Lewis prepared a new argument "in resistance to Defendant's Demurrer." It exceeded 130 pages in length and is of interest primarily because it had to exclude virtually any mention—let alone discussion and explanation—of the historical claims and alleged facts that had made up the bulk of his earlier petition. For now the Okanogan and Colville grievances would have to be put on hold. In fact, unless Lewis was to prevail concerning the matter of the demurrer, in the context of S. 3185 they would simply be irrelevant.

Lewis opened his brief with a blunt assertion that the right to retain and ultimately "pocket veto" a bill duly passed by the Congress "raises a question here that demands immediate settlement, both in the interests of the parties to this action, and of the Congress and the Executive, either of whom may be deprived of lawful authority vested by the Constitution unless the balance between these two branches of government be kept true and adjusted on a proper and established basis." Which construction should prevail—"Executive or Congressional?" He also mentioned the discussion in the House earlier in February 1927. Of course, he conceded, "the action of the House is [not] in any way binding on this Court . . . but on account of the high legal standing and reputation of the members of the House Committee," Lewis cited the report and legislative interpretation presented by it "in support of the construction here urged by the Petitioners."

Counsel further pointed to "the necessity that the Courts now act before the initiation of an alleged unfounded Executive authority may be deemed to have established an unconstitutional practice in derogation of rights and powers of Congress." This case, Lewis added, "irrespective of the Interests of the Petitioners" (and a few lines later, Lewis noted that some "thirteen millions of dollars" were involved), "presents a legal question of extreme importance and gravity." Rare is the appellate attorney who will not argue that his/her case represents a legal question "of extreme importance and gravity." On the other hand, perhaps Lewis can be pardoned for urging that the matter in which he had been occupied for between three and four years and which concerned major questions of justice, equity, and possible long-term wrongdoing by the federal government might well merit such a description. His case raises an issue of

> asserted constitutional departure and violation that may be far reaching in its effects in the future; both on the Congress whose authority to override a veto is set at naught, and on the Executive, whose legislative power for securing revision of pending legislation may be curtailed by the repudiation of any ability to return such legislation to the Congress . . . should the Houses thereof be in recess at the end of the ten day period. Unsettled, the question might arise regarding the status of subsequent enactments affecting millions of dollars, and the most vital matters of government.

Early in his brief, Lewis presented two key points that he would repeatedly emphasize throughout his lengthy presentation. (1) "The only adjournment that can prevent a return of the bill is the final adjournment of the Congress." Under this construction, the type of adjournment that had taken place in the case of S. 3185 would not qualify for the silent pocket veto utilized by Coolidge. As Hatton Sumners had emphasized, the House had adjourned only to a specific date in the future when it would return for a second session of the same Congress. (2) The corollary to this point is the argument raised by the government that the president can return a bill to the relevant House "only while the Congress is in active session." According to Lewis, if the House adjourns within ten days of a bill's passage, the president can pocket veto "bills theretofore regularly passed and so presented," regardless of the fact that "the same Congress is to reconvene thereafter for further consideration of the legislation yet pending or that may be brought before it."

Lewis proceeded to cite and discuss a number of state cases in which he sought to demonstrate that some tribunals had distinguished between "recess" and "adjournment." Moreover, at least one court had held that "the provisions of [a state] constitution apply to adjournments *sine die*, and not to adjournments from time to time." Such a holding would, of course, vindicate his key contention just noted. But counsel for petitioners had additional arguments to present on this issue, even as he had to confront a difficult challenge concerning application of the pocket veto.

It was one thing to declare its application as unwarranted by the Constitution. It was quite another matter, however, to rebut the irrefutable fact that the vast majority of presidents from James Madison to Calvin Coolidge had utilized the practice. Lewis proposed to attack as unlawful what had become commonplace in executive administrations for more than a century.

He began this section of his brief with the subtitle "Precedents not a First or Best Guide to Construction," and this after spending the last twenty pages or so searching for them. Such was not an unusual contradiction. Many if not most appellate attorneys have not hesitated to attack the old doctrine of stare decisis (application of precedent), all the more when its application would defeat their argument. Yet counsel insisted that "the recognized rules of interpretation require that construction of the Constitution be made, if possible, from the language of the instrument itself." In arguing that a congressional adjournment strictly meant only a final conclusion and not the temporary cessation of one session to be followed by another in due course, William Lewis maintained that because Congress had not finally adjourned in 1926, Coolidge had been at perfect liberty to submit his objections to the legislature within the ten-day framework. Nothing but his own inclinations had prevented him from doing so.

For Lewis, this view represented exactly the type of construction he had just described: "one that gives full force and meaning to its language; which is in perfect harmony with the purpose of the general veto clause and of the ten day provision . . . ; which is not in derogation of any of the rights of the Congress or of the Executive, and which *is in harmony with* the intent and purpose of the people who framed and adopted the Constitution." Moreover, the fact that legal objection to the pocket veto at the federal level had not yet materialized was not important. In reality,

acquiescence or sufferance for no length of time can legalize a clear usurpation of power. . . . A claim of power is frequently permitted or yielded to merely because it is claimed, and it may be exercised for a long period in absence of any constitutional right or power, and even in violation of constitutional prohibition without special occasion arising for its interpretation by a court, or any one being sufficiently interested in the subject to raise the question.

In this case, counsel observed, the Indigenous tribes and the United States have put forward two very different constructions of the constitutional provision relating to the pocket veto. In determining the correct one, he asserted that "the plain language of the Constitution itself is the best guide to the construction of this clause."

The US attorney had insisted that if the framers had meant by "adjournment" a final adjournment, they would have plainly so stated. By the same token, added Lewis, if the framers had intended the word to apply to an adjournment of a session, "they would also have plainly so stated." The key to the correct interpretation of the clause for Lewis was *not* the word "adjournment" but rather the word "prevent." It was "the wholly unconstitutional practice of [the] silent pocket veto" (except in the case of an adjournment *sine die*), which, Lewis added, had been repudiated by the House in February 1927. It was unconstitutional because in practice, the pocket veto failed to recognize "the clear constitutional right of the Congress to receive a written statement of the Executive's veto objections," a right violated by Coolidge in his recent veto of S. 3185.

Much of the main section of Lewis's brief expanded on this point. He claimed, for example, that it is a misinterpretation of the Constitution to permit an extension of the "Executive veto power by way of silent and absolute pocket veto," except and only except when both houses of Congress have adjourned *sine die*. The confessed object and purpose of the veto, he added, "is the return of the legislation for its reconsideration or revision . . . in connection with specific objections made thereto by the President." With one exception these two functions must accompany each other. The *only* exception is the adjournment *sine die*. Although the framers declined to give the president an absolute veto, in effect the silent pocket veto does just that. Without comment, explanation, or opportunity for congressional reconsideration—without doing anything, in reality as far as the particular bill is concerned—the chief executive can exercise total control. Thus the pocket veto "gives to his inaction, greater force and power than to his action. It makes of silence a greater power than voice." Lewis insisted that such was never the intention of the framers.

Counsel reminded the judges that "a constitution is to be considered as a whole and all portions must be harmonized if possible[,] and where a constitutional provision will bear two constructions [as in the present case] one of which is consistent with, and the other inconsistent with an intention expressed in a previous section, the former must be adopted that both provisions may stand and have effect." He summed up his brief by emphasizing anew that "a holding that the return may be made to the Congress though not in active session, [but in a case wherein] the Congress has not finally adjourned, is the only conclusion that preserves the true balance, rights, powers, and duties of all." On January 9, 1928, the case was argued before the Court of Claims, and both parties anticipated the decision of the judges. They only had a few months to wait.

*　*　*

Court of Claims chief judge Edward Campbell delivered his court's unanimous opinion in *Okanogan . . . Indians et al. v. United States* on April 16, 1928. He readily sustained the demurrer. If William Lewis had hoped for some judicial consideration, if not explication of the issues he had raised, he must have been disappointed. Not counting the traditional introductory recitation of the facts in the case, Campbell's opinion came to barely four and a half pages in length. Depending on one's viewpoint, it might be described as either a workable synthesis of superficiality or a model of conciseness. As for Lewis's efforts, Campbell dismissed them in one sentence. "With great industry counsel for the parties have produced historical precedents and decisions by State courts supposed to bear upon or decide similar questions." He failed to cite, let alone consider, any one of them in his decision.

Indeed, Campbell gave little indication that he had taken the Lewis petition and brief into serious consideration. He wrote of Lewis that "the plaintiff's contention would seem to imply that the [constitutional] provision 'if any bill shall not be returned by the President within ten days . . . the same shall be a law.'" But, added Campbell, "the contention disregards the following phrase, 'unless the Congress by their adjournment prevents the return, in which case it shall not become a law.'" The chief judge asserted further that "the contention here is that the bill [S. 3185] became a law because the adjournment of the Congress . . . was only an adjournment of the 1st session of the 69th Congress, and the President did not return the bill to the Congress . . . or . . . to officers or employee of the House or Senate who may have . . . kept it until the Congress was again in session." Moreover, "it is manifest that he should have lodged it with these officers or employees within that period," assuming that Lewis's "contention have any merit." However, "it is also manifest that . . . there is no merit in the contention."

In a few sentences the chief judge dismissed Lewis's arguments. "Transmitting the bill to either employees or to the next session," he wrote, "will not vitalize a bill that upon adjournment the Constitution declares shall not be a law." Further, "the attempted distinction between adjournment of one or the other session is unsound." According to Campbell, "the Constitution does not limit the time of adjournment to the final adjournment at the second session [as Lewis had insisted], and the courts have no right to so limit it." In other words, when the first session of the Sixty-Ninth Congress adjourned, in the midst of the ten-day period, "that was an adjournment of the Congress." Therefore Coolidge had been under no constitutional obligation to do or not do anything concerning S. 3185. While previous presidents had called attention to the fact that a bill had failed to become a law, "we do not find a provision requiring the President" to do so.

Prior to his next public step, William Lewis and his co-counsel, John Carter, subjected Campbell's decision to a line-by-line analysis. Apparently they were less than impressed. Where Campbell had written that the plaintiff "disregards" the constitutional provision relating to adjournment, Carter had noted that "plaintiffs contention implied no such thing." Campbell's statement "begs the question." As to the chief judge's further comment that unless the key constitutional clause is ignored, there is no merit in Lewis's contention, Carter found this to be simply "a Non Sequitur," which once again "begs the question." Further, why is Lewis's distinction between one type of adjournment or another "unsound"? Simply because Campbell says so? His sentence is nothing more than an example of ipse dixit. It is "valid because I said it." No further citation was apparently necessary. Surely Lewis's argument deserved more than this. It "is a major issue of the case," and all Campbell seemed inclined to do was dismiss it "with a declarative sentence." Indeed, the "Constitution is silent as to [the] meaning of the word adjournment, which is to be construed according to usage, rules of Congress, precedents, and court decisions, which is just what the Court has not done thus far."

Finally, Lewis's associates noted that the one case that Campbell did cite, the *La Abra Silver Mining* opinion noted above, was really irrelevant because it involved a statute that had been signed by the president during a congressional recess. Such had not been the case with S. 3185, which had been pocket vetoed. Campbell had mentioned Madison's famous pocket veto of 1812. "This is only Madison's opinion of the Constitutional effect of the adjournment of the session. Congress, not the President should be the judge of its own rules, customs and procedure. A constructional construction long adhered to, will not be overthrown." At some point after the digest had been prepared, William Lewis decided on the next step. The Colville and Okanogan tribes would ask the Court of Claims for a new trial.

He filed the printed petition for "a rehearing and new trial" on June 9, 1928, and based it on a number of "errors in law" found in Campbell's April 16 unanimous decision sustaining the government's demurrer. In the first place, Campbell had failed "to give full and due consideration and weight" to the fact that the Constitution's veto provisions at issue here "were derived from existing State constitutions." While Campbell acknowledged that Lewis had listed a number of such cases, the chief judge neither cited nor analyzed any of them. Yet they had been "rendered on the same question and under identical constitutional provisions." Further, Campbell had failed to grasp the fact that the purpose of the veto provision "is to permit the *revision*, not the defeat of legislation by the President."

In fact, the court's decision "gives the President's silence and inaction greater force and power than the Constitution expressly confers on his written objections returned with a bill." Not only does it deprive the Congress of the right to "receive and know the President's specific written objections to legislation duly passed," but also it deprives the Congress "and therefore the people of their right and opportunity to consider the President's objections and to revise the bill to conform therewith," or to override the veto. In truth, under the pocket veto, with neither explanation nor justification but just mere silence, the president can kill a statute duly enacted by Congress. Campbell had also ruled that the Constitution required a return of a bill from the president to a house "in active legislative session." According to the wording in the document, however, the Constitution "places no such restriction upon either the President or the Congress." Examination of the clause in question indicates that counsel for the tribes was correct.

William Lewis expanded on these points in a "Supplemental Brief on

Motion for a New Trial." He quoted Campbell's statement that Lewis had "produced historical precedents and decisions by State courts supposed to bear upon or decide similar questions." In effect, Campbell himself had demurred, in that he figuratively had asked "So what?" Lewis returned the serve, as it were. "It is the insistence of Petitioners [and Lewis gave the legal citations for ten such state cases] that these authorities pass upon and decide the identical question now before this Court, as arising under State constitutions containing the identical quoted language." They "are unanimous in holding that the adjournment of the legislature contemplated in the quoted clause of the constitution is a final adjournment." Further, "there being no Federal decisions on the question, great weight should be given to judicial construction of identical language in State Constitutions by the courts of the several states cited by Petitioners."

As to Campbell's insistence that Lewis had "ignored and disregarded the language of this exception clause," Lewis responded that "it is Petitioners' insistence that their entire Brief and argument is devoted to analysis and construction of the language of this particular clause, and that this Court . . . should give full and due consideration to the purpose and intent of this Constitutional provision." It was never intended under the Constitution, he added, "that the Executive should, by withholding a bill, defeat legislation." Indeed, "it was never the intention of those who framed the Constitution that the fate of legislation should lie with one man, the Executive, but always with the Congress." Finally, Lewis reiterated a point he had made at the conclusion of his first brief to the Court of Claims. "Contemporary or subsequent construction," he insisted, "can never abrogate the text of a constitution; it can never fritter away its obvious sense; it can never narrow down its true limitations; it can never enlarge its true boundaries." Therefore, there was no place in sound constitutional construction for a pocket veto.

On October 15 the Court of Claims heard the re-argument in the Colville and Okanogan case. Again William Lewis represented the tribes, although their claims of alleged injustices had long since ceased to play any part in the litigation. Attorney William Norris represented the United States. The Carter Papers contain what appears to be a stenographic typescript of the oral presentations delivered in court on that day. It makes interesting reading.

Lewis spent much of his time calling for a construction of the Constitution that uses "a common sense meaning to its words." No one assumes, he observed, that when Congress is required to present an enacted bill to the president, "the whole Congress shall suspend and go up in a body" to the White House. In fact, the bill "is sent up, or taken up." A clerk at the White House signs a receipt for it "and lays it upon the desk of the President for his attention." If a bill can be presented to the chief executive in such a manner, one that "accords with common sense construction," it can be returned "in the same manner." It may be received at the appropriate house "by one of its agents, the Clerk, the Speaker, the Secretary or the President Pro Tem," and that despite the fact that the House is not actually sitting, but is in recess over the week-end, for the holidays, or is in recess between the sessions, and will be held "for consideration at its next regular meeting."

Lewis echoed a few points that he had already submitted to the court in his supplemental brief. The ten-day rule "never was intended to serve the President as a means to defeat the right of Congress to consider [a] bill with the President's objection, or to defeat the rights of Congress to take periodic recesses or adjournments." In fact, "the Congress exists as a political body for the two year period of its existence, and may . . . meet at any time it wishes to, or remain throughout in continuous session. There is nothing in the Constitution to the contrary." Counsel reminded the court that "legislative power under the Constitution is solely under Congress." The president's "authority is advisory and revisory. He cannot legislate." Although Lewis chose not to be more explicit, he seems to have been implying that by employing the pocket veto, the president comes close, perhaps too close, to impinging on the legislative prerogative.

For his part, William Norris recalled to Lewis that one of his grounds for a new trial had been that only three judges heard his original case, with a fourth joining in Campbell's decision. Norris could not resist reminding "my young friend" that he had been "asked by the Chief Judge if he wished to argue the matter before the number of judges then present, and he consented to do so." Given the fact that ultimately four out of five judges participated in a unanimous decision, it is not clear what Lewis hoped to gain in seeking an en banc rehearing. Apparently, Norris did not pursue this issue. Rather, he emphasized the importance of James Madison to the government's case.

He was, according to Norris, "one of the framers . . . and certainly must have known what the framers of that instrument intended by its various provisions." Moreover,

> a great many of the Presidents, in fact almost all of them, including Abraham Lincoln, Woodrow Wilson, Warren Harding, Calvin Coolidge, and our present Chief Justice Mr. Taft thought that they were within their rights under the Constitution in considering that if the session of Congress had adjourned within the ten day period prescribed, that they could not, and were prevented thereby from returning a bill with objections to the Congress, and that therefore it did not become a law. . . . Is it possible that they were all wrong in this respect, including Madison, one of the framers of the Constitution? When, on the other hand, has there been any opposition to this practice, by Congress, or elsewhere?

To ask the question, according to Norris, was to answer it. Norris offered no indication, however, that he was familiar with the House colloquy on February 26, 1927, concerning the pocket veto.

One week after the re-argument, on October 22, 1928, the Court of Claims overruled—apparently without written opinion—Lewis's motion for a new hearing. It thereby left the Okanogan and Colville tribes where they had been before he filed his original petition more than a year earlier. If he wanted to pursue his case any further, counsel for the tribes had two options remaining. Either he could work to get another jurisdictional statute through Congress, an uncertain if not tortuous course at best, even though Coolidge probably would have left the presidency by the time the bill reached the White House, or Lewis could ask the US Supreme Court to hear the case. In the past he had emphasized that the high court had never accepted a case on the legitimacy of the pocket veto. In this case, however, Lewis as well as the House Committee on the Judiciary had presented a clear constitutional challenge to it. Surely this issue was now ripe for a definitive judicial resolution and one possibly in favor of the tribes—or so Lewis hoped.

CHAPTER 5

The Supreme Court Agrees to Read and Listen, 1928–1929

It does not come as a surprise to learn that in December 1928 William Lewis prepared to seek a writ of certiorari from the Supreme Court. Having already been turned down by a unanimous Court of Claims, if he wanted to continue his battle in court, he had little choice. His request, still on behalf of the tribes, appeared in three different forums, and each one was more extensive than that which preceded it. On December 4 he filed his first petition, which listed nine points to justify the grant from the high court, on a question "of great public interest and far reaching importance." Stripped of their legal verbiage, four should be noted here.

In the first place, the justices needed to construe the meaning of the phrase "by their adjournment prevent its return." Did the word "adjournment" refer to a final adjournment of Congress, or to adjournment of a session of Congress either from day to day or for longer periods of time? Further, did adjournment prevent the return of a bill by the president replete with his objections thereto? Were the ten days referred to in the Constitution calendar days or legislative days? Beyond answering these queries, Lewis asked the justices to consider several additional issues.

"It would appear," Lewis wrote, "to be the constitutional duty of the President to afford Congress an opportunity to consider his objections to all bills passed by it . . . before the final adjournment of any particular Congress." By his action in 1926, Coolidge had deprived Congress of such an opportunity. Such a step "appears to be in conflict" with congressional authority for "the exclusive right to legislate." It represents "an absolute veto," a power the president does not possess. The veto in question denies Congress "its constitutional right to repass identical legislation by a two-thirds vote and thus make it a law not withstanding any executive objections." Because this case "necessitates the final determination of the line of demarcation between the Executive and Legislative Branches of the government," the case at bar "should be determined by this Court as the Court of last resort." Finally, Lewis stated that since the judiciary committees of both the House and Senate had at different times disagreed with various presidents on an interpretation of the Constitution's veto clause, "it is considered of the utmost importance that this provision should be construed by this Honorable Court."

Within a matter of weeks, Lewis expanded his original petition with a brief filed in support of it. In it, he again included his list of "errors" allegedly committed by the Court of Claims as summarized in his earlier request for a rehearing. The lower tribunal had not considered constitutional language that in effect required the president "to return the bill with his [written] objections" prior to any final adjournment by Congress. Moreover, it had erred in "not giving due consideration to the formal protests against the Presidential use of the pocket veto" by the House Committee on the Judiciary. It had deprived the lawmakers of their right to receive written explanations from the president concerning objections to a particular bill, as well as the opportunity to respond to them.

Lewis asked the justices to consider that "the enjoyment of our right to life, liberty, and the pursuit of happiness is circumscribed and regulated by the laws passed by Congress. Consequently, any question growing out of a conflict of authority between the President and the Congress . . . is of such great public importance as to fully justify" consideration by the Supreme Court. Also, it was essential that the tribunal "finally construe and define" the constitutional meaning of the term "adjournment." In particular, what appropriate application of the word "will prevent the return by the President with his objections of a bill which has been duly passed?" Further, if the power to legislate rested totally in the hands of Congress, how could the chief executive deny Congress both the right to enact a bill and the opportunity to learn from and consider any objections he might have to the measure? When and where did authority to legislate and authority to negative collide, and what was the appropriate outcome?

The first brief submitted by the United States in response to the

Lewis petition for certiorari came to all of two and a half pages. But it mentioned a new document unexpectedly transmitted to the House by President Coolidge, on December 22, 1928, without a single word of explanation, as was his wont. Instead, accompanying the "Report on the Pocket Veto" was merely a single sentence from Coolidge: "I am transmitting herewith for the information of the Congress a memorandum prepared in the office of the Attorney General regarding bills presented to the President less than ten days before the adjournment of Congress and not signed by him." All parties to this appeal—Lewis, the solicitor general, the amicus curiae, and finally the Supreme Court itself—in their own way would respond to it. For now, William Mitchell, the solicitor general, simply observed that "the question is an important one and should be settled by this Court. For that reason, the United States concurs in the petition for certiorari."

On January 21, 1929, the high court granted the writ. Since passage of the "Judges' Bill" in 1925, the court has been given almost total discretion over its docket. Why it granted "cert" in this case remains unclear. There seems little doubt that the congressional position concerning the pocket veto was at odds with existing executive practice. Thus, if only to settle the issue, allowing the writ to issue becomes understandable. As a collective body, however, the justices do not explain why they either grant or decline to grant a writ of certiorari, although individual justices may sometimes clarify why they would have permitted the writ, especially in cases where the application has not received the required four votes in order to go forward. Here, William Lewis had presented a variety of compelling reasons why the matter of the pocket veto deserved Supreme Court scrutiny. Further, the United States had concurred, urging upon the justices the necessity for gaining judicial resolution of the issue. It would appear that the vote to grant "cert" was unanimous.

* * *

By 1929, William Lewis had been practicing law for more than thirty years, having graduated from Stanford University and been admitted to the Washington State bar at the age of twenty-two in 1898. Further, he was quite familiar with the various nuances of representing Indigenous clients on the reservations. As he prepared to submit his final brief representing the Okanogan and Colville tribes, one suspects that he could only have been well aware of the very serious obstacles looming along the route to a favorable holding. Not only had the Court of Claims been unanimous against him, but also the brief for the government could make good use of the *Report on the Pocket Veto*, drafted in the attorney general's office and compiled by one of the government attorneys who would participate in the forthcoming oral argument before the nine justices.

Lewis had every reason to be concerned about this compilation of more than one hundred specific instances in which presidents from Madison to Coolidge had employed the pocket veto at the end of a (not final) session of Congress, to say nothing of the apparent suddenness with which Coolidge had forwarded the report to Congress. This was not an instance in which counsel could dispute or refute the facts. In this case they were virtually irrefutable. For the most part, the bills that had been enacted were still available in the Executive Office, where Robert Reeder had identified and examined them. Further, as the practice of the pocket veto had continued unabated, especially in the decades after the Civil War, the well-established doctrine of stare decisis became more influential and important.

Meaning "to stand by what is decided," the maxim increasingly came to imply acceptance of what had been adjudicated previously, even if in a new context it might be rejected. In short, the heavy hand of more than a century's legal history of the pocket veto confronted Lewis. It would be difficult to rebut, although not impossible. Moreover, there were some other related legal questions that counsel intended to raise that might undercut the effectiveness of stare decisis. Finally, counsel for the tribes looked forward to the final opportunity to draw on his earlier submissions, to synthesize and reiterate his key points anew. His brief of more than fifty pages was the result. On the whole, it represents his most thorough and thoughtful critique of the pocket veto.

At the outset, Lewis asserted that his case "involves an original construction of the Constitution" and calls for resolution of the difference in construction between the executive and the legislature "with respect to the correct interpretation . . . of [its] veto provisions." For the third time he emphasized that "the legal question" involved is "of importance far beyond the present case." Two questions directly related to the constitutionality of the pocket veto required definitive answers: (1) if there are different meanings to the word "adjournment," and (2) "whether the adjournment of the 69th Congress for [its] customary summer recess on July 3, 1926—eight days after the bill S 3185 was submitted to the President—prevented [his] return of the bill within ten days to the House." The key constitutional phrase, added counsel, is "Unless the Congress by their adjournment prevent its return, in which case it shall not be a law." Lewis then repeated his list of the various errors supposedly committed by the Court of Claims in its earlier decision sustaining the government's demurrer. They "all relate to the proper method, the proper aids, and the proper tests by which [a] correct constitutional construction may be attained, and whereby an incorrect construction may be detected and rejected."

Lewis set forth a claim he repeated several times in his brief, that "the distinction between all adjournments of the Congress (other than final adjournment) is one of duration and nomenclature only." When the legislature returned from its summer recess, they resumed their business "precisely where it left off, without any difference occasioned by duration of the recess." This point is important for Lewis, because the Constitution's language refers to adjournment and not a recess. He would insist at numerous points that even though the lawmakers had recessed, Congress was still technically in session, and by failing to return the bill with his written objections, Coolidge had violated the Constitution. Furthermore, the section at issue is not whether Congress adjourns but rather "unless the Congress prevent its return by their adjournment." In other words, what type of adjournment would "prevent" its return?

Early in his brief, the lawyer for the tribes insisted that while there were at least four different types of adjournment, only one—a final adjournment—would prevent the president from returning the bill within ten days with his written objections. What type of adjournment, in other words, is one "that will prevent its return"? He cautioned the justices that "the presumption is that a definite meaning attaches to each word, and where the words employed ... embody a definite meaning which involves no conflict with other parts of the Constitution, the meaning thus apparent on its face must be adopted, and it is not within the province of the Court to speculate otherwise as to the purpose of the framers." Thus the meaning of the only type of adjournment to fit this description is "final adjournment." By the common rules of statutory construction, other types of adjournment such as per diem or summer recess are excluded.

This means, according to Lewis, that when Congress recessed for the summer in July 1926, its adjournment did not fall within the exception clause. Therefore, with the Sixty-Ninth Congress not in session but still in existence, "the bill must be constructively returned to that House, during its temporary recess, by delivery to the presiding or recording officers thereof" during the ten-day period, or "else the bill becomes a law." Thus no constitutional justification existed for Coolidge's failure to return the bill with his written objections. Such was the underlying assumption that undergirded the petitioner's brief.

Moreover, and contrary to the position taken by the United States, Lewis found "no constitutional requirements" either that the veto be exercised only during "the active legislative sitting of the Congress" or that the bill be returned "only during the active legislative session," or that "the returned bill and veto must be received and acted upon during the same session of the Congress at which the bill was passed." Indeed, he insisted that "it was never the intention [of the framers] that the President's inaction should in any way defeat such legislation." Hence it would appear "to be the constitutional duty of the President" to afford the Congress an opportunity to consider his written objections to a bill, subject only to a final adjournment of the Congress. Implementing a pocket veto "confers upon the Executive an absolute veto power," something that is not authorized anywhere in the Constitution. There is, further, "no conceivable way in which the President's duty" to return a bill "is in any way altered or affected by a recess" where the adjournments are temporary and both houses may later "reassemble and sit after the adjournment and resume their interrupted legislative programs." The interpretation of adjournment insisted on by Lewis contrasted with that of the United States to the effect that "any adjournment of the Congress existing at the expiration of the allotted ten days *ipso facto* prevents an unreturned bill from becoming a law."

While Lewis appeared to concede the existence of the pocket veto if Congress had initiated a final adjournment during the ten-day period as mandated by the Constitution, even in this instance he raised constitutional objections to the practice. However, according to him, the government went much further. It was one thing for Congress to forfeit its right to receive and react to written executive objections concerning a proposed statute when it had initiated a final adjournment. It was quite another to apply the practice to all kinds of legislative interruption—thus making a bad situation so much the worse. Accepting presidential inaction and executive silence as legitimate gives the chief executive "greater power than . . . his expressed objections returned to Congress with the bill."

Saying and doing nothing "in effect gives to the President an absolute veto power which was clearly denied him by the Constitution." Congress is denied not only the right to learn the reasons for the executive objections but also the opportunity to respond to them. "Absolute veto power, based upon the return of a bill, is wholly unknown under any constitution, State or Federal, under which we live, and such a veto can under no circumstances be upheld without doing violence to both the letter and the spirit of the Constitution. No absolute veto should be upheld, based upon failure to return a bill during the legislative existence of the Congress." (Inexplicably, Lewis ignored the very difficult issue of whether Congress was in legislative existence when in actual fact it was absent.) In sum, the constitutional construction adopted by the Court of Claims and urged on the Supreme Court gives no consideration to the policy of the framers "that the will of the Congress should be supreme." It "deprives the Congress unnecessarily of its exclusive right to legislate, prevents any revision, and clothes the President with an absolute veto." All of this, according to Lewis, is contrary to what the framers intended and adopted.

At this point in his brief, counsel for the tribes confronted the implications of the report on the pocket veto that had been sent to the House by President Coolidge in December. While he declined to cite or mention the report directly, its relevance for his comments is unmistakable. Lewis began by emphasizing that "it is a primary function of Congress to make the laws, the Judiciary to interpret them, and the Executive to administer them." Thus it is for the courts and the courts alone to construe the Constitution. Precedents (and here Lewis is referring indirectly to the more than a hundred previous instances of the pocket veto cited in the report) "are not a first or best guide for construction." Indeed, "neither construction nor precedents of construction . . . [can] override the clear meaning and plain intent of the Constitutional language."

Counsel offered some insights on constitutional construction, drawing on well-established texts by Joseph Story and Thomas Cooley.

Precedents, he emphasized, "cannot abrogate the provisions of the Constitution." Indeed, "contemporary or subsequent construction can never" do this. "It can never fritter away its obvious sense," nor "narrow down its true limitations," nor "enlarge its true boundaries." A claim of constitutional authority "is frequently permitted or yielded to merely because it is claimed, and it may be exercised over a long period of time." Such circumstances, however, "can not be allowed to sanction a clear infraction of the Constitution, or the neglect to discharge constitutional duties or the disregard of the clear right of the Congress." All three of these actions had occurred whenever the pocket veto was exercised in the absence of a final adjournment.

Therefore, Lewis insisted, "Neither the President nor Congress can by action or precedence or concurrence therein, alter the plain language or defeat this clear intent and purpose of the Constitution." Moreover, it makes no difference if Congress by its silence has acquiesced in such action "when the judicial branch . . . alone has been vested with the power to determine whether or not . . . a bill so ignored or pocket vetoed has become a law. And this is the precise reason for the case at bar." Thus, no matter how often "the Executive has asserted the right of pocket veto, or Congress has or has not so acquiesced in [its use] in the past, is entirely immaterial, for the policy, the purpose, the plain language and clear intent of the Constitution is controlling." In fact, what the government has presented is nothing less than "a gradual development of asserted and unconstitutional Executive power."

William Lewis summarized his argument by citing four specific constitutional violations incurred whenever the pocket veto was exercised: "(1) It is an unwarranted interference with the exclusive legislative power of Congress. (2) It prevents consideration by Congress of the reasons [why] the legislation is objectionable to the Executive. (3) It prevents such corrective modification of the legislation as may commend itself to the mind of Congress. (4) It constitutes an absolute prohibition against such legislation by the Executive, who is denied that power by the Constitution."

Finally, Lewis reminded the court once again that "it was never intended . . . that the Executive should, by withholding a bill, defeat legislation." But such has been the result from the pocket veto. When Congress had recessed for the summer in July 1926, such action "was not a final adjournment," nor did it relieve the president from his obligation to make return of the bill within ten days, nor did it "prevent the return of the bill within the true meaning and intent of the Constitution." Thus S.·3185 was and remained an existing law. The decision of the Court of Claims to the contrary should be reversed, and the government should be required "to answer to the petition."

* * *

The brief for the United States, with due allowance for the usual statement of facts, came to about half the length of Lewis's argument. Both Lewis and the solicitor general, William Mitchell—for whom the future held appointment as attorney general by Herbert Hoover—were in agreement concerning the facts of the case, as well as the key questions to be presented to the justices. Such an outward consensus, however, should not lead the reader to underestimate the basic dispute concerning the "correct" interpretation of the veto clause in the Constitution. Moreover, Mitchell may well have had one advantage over Lewis in that arguing over what is as contrasted with what one party to the litigation thinks should be sometimes represents an easier challenge for the litigant.

At the outset, Mitchell recalled that the New York Constitution had included a clause stating that if adjournment rendered the return of a bill impracticable, "it shall be returned on the first day of the meeting of the legislature after the expiration of the said ten days." He observed, however, that the framers had deliberately omitted this clause from the federal Constitution. Mitchell added that the ten-day requirement, excluding Sundays, "means ten calendar days," and the "exception of Sundays show[s] that every other day is to be counted." Here, using a traditional canon of statutory interpretation, he claimed that the specific mention of Sunday implied exclusion of all the other days from the limitation. Thus a return prevented by adjournment is simply a return within ten calendar days, Sundays excepted.

There was also "no basis for limiting the application of the word 'adjournment' to an adjournment at the end of a Congress." The framers used the word "in the broad sense." Contrary to the position taken by Lewis, if Congress chooses to adjourn and this decision falls within the ten-day period, such action results from the choice of the legislators.

Congress loses its opportunity to pass a bill over the President's disapproval by not being in session on the tenth day following presentation to the President if he fails to return it. Indeed, the pocket veto comes to life only when Congress adjourns.

The solicitor general gave another point emphasized by Lewis equally short shrift. Acceptance of the claim that the president could return the bill "to some officer of the adjourned House, to be retained in his custody until Congress reassembles," has no basis in law. "No Act has ever been passed authorizing any officer of either House to so receive returned bills, and there is no rule of either House giving such authority." In fact, the return must be made to the house and not to an officer. "The word House as used in the Constitution has always been held to mean the House in session," and no message from the chief executive is received "except by a House in session."

William Lewis had possibly tried to limit the impact of the report from the attorney general's office concerning the pocket veto by never referring to it directly. Not so with William Mitchell. He concluded the first part of his brief with the direct statement that "the practical construction given to this clause in the Constitution is controlling." He would have further specific reference to it later on, but for now he wrote that since 1789 "there have been 120 cases like this of so called pocket vetoes." In none of them, until the recent action by the House in the Sixty-Ninth Congress, had "any action been taken by Presidents or Congress" based on Lewis's theory. Most important, "in none of the 120 cases referred to has any of the pocketed measures been placed upon the statute books or treated as a law." Not until the singular attempt related to S. 3185. As a later song made popular by the Beatles would say, essentially Mitchell urged the justices to "let it be."

The next section of Mitchell's brief expanded on the points just mentioned, although it would appear that in barely two pages he had seriously damaged the claims put forth by William Lewis. It was true, he conceded, that the exception clause in the veto section of the federal Constitution had been based on that of New York. It was also true that the state's provision mandated that a bill would become a law in ten days unless rendered impractical by adjournment, "in which case the bill shall be returned on the first day of the meeting of the legislature after the expiration of the said ten days." Had this clause been part of the 1787 document, in 1926 the fate of S. 3185 might well have been very different. But it was deleted in the final version sent to the states for ratification.

Not only had the framers declined to include the provision of the New York Constitution "that in case of adjournment the bill might be returned on the first day of the next session," but also in 1822, the New York constitutional convention deleted it as well, thereby making New York's language concerning the veto virtually identical to that of the federal Constitution. Thus constitutional language that conceivably could have aided Lewis is conspicuous by its absence. In a similar vein, Mitchell disposed of his claim that ten days could mean ten legislative days. But "the Framers did not say that." The constitutional language simply means that "the return by the President must be made within ten calendar days, Sundays excepted."

What of Lewis's insistence that a bill could be returned to an officer of the House or Senate, in the absence of the legislature? Again, "the framers did not say that." Rather, "the bill shall be returned to the 'House' in which it shall have originated." Returning a bill "to an officer of either House after adjournment of Congress is not returning the bill to the Congress," which is the constitutional mandate. Moreover, Mitchell added that "it has been the universal practice of . . . Congress to receive messages from the President . . . only while in session." In short, "if it is not legally possible to return a bill to a House not in session, it is plain that [Lewis's] argument must be rejected."

Mitchell also had a few words for the House Committee on the Judiciary, which, it will be recalled, had voted that in spite of a pocket veto, a bill not appropriately returned to the House had indeed become a law. "We have," he observed, "the utmost deference for the view of the learned members of the Judiciary Committee." However, "if there had been presented to [it] the constitutional difficulties in the way of returning a bill to a House not in session," as well as the "overwhelming practical construction of the Constitution" afterwards disclosed, "the Committee's conclusion would have been the other way." Indeed, the bulk of Mitchell's remaining argument focused on the document submitted to the House by President Coolidge on December 22, 1928. The president referred to it as "a memorandum prepared in the office of the Attorney General regarding bills presented to the President less than ten days before the adjournment of Congress and not signed by him." Its author, Justice Department staff attorney Robert Reeder, had sought to answer the question, "In the case of each such bill, what was done with the engrossed copy of the bill, and what communication or memorandum was made in connection with such disposition?"

Extending to more than forty pages, Robert Reeder's "memorandum" apparently located and identified every instance of a pocket veto, beginning with the presidency of James Madison and ending with 1928, the final year of Coolidge's term. Dated October 10, 1928, it remains unclear as to when the attorney general submitted the document to Coolidge. We know, however, that he transmitted it to the House on December 22. All parties to the case were able to draw on it as they prepared their briefs for submission to the Supreme Court. The difference between Lewis and Mitchell in their use of the "House Report on Pocket Veto" is striking and warrants some discussion.

For reasons that remain unclear, possibly because Reeder had assembled such an exhaustive, lengthy, and consistent compilation concerning use of the pocket veto, Lewis declined specifically to refer to it in his brief. Neither could he hope to refute the evidence compiled in it. Rather, he sought to attack the significance of the memorandum by indirection. He insisted that lengthy repetition of an unconstitutional and improper practice was not significant. Such extensive use, therefore, neither contributed to its supposed legitimacy nor in any way justified its continuation—all the more as the high court had thus far in its history failed to consider the specific legal question.

As solicitor general, William Mitchell found the appearance of Reeder's memorandum fraught with significance. One suspects he had long been aware of its preparation, if only because Robert Reeder appears as a cosigner of the government's brief in the pocket veto case. Mitchell gave the section of his brief dealing with the memorandum the title that "the practical construction is controlling, and it completely sustains the Respondent's position." The document showed "the results of an exhaustive research of governmental archives, for the purpose of disclosing the practical construction placed upon the constitutional provisions here involved." Not only did it cover "so called pocket vetoes at the final sessions of the Congress," but also "those at ad interim adjournments of sessions," such as the one involved in this case. The scope of Reeder's research appeared to be very thorough.

Reeder identified and located at least 120 pocket vetoes that had taken place fewer than ten days "before an adjournment which did not mark the end of that Congress." While in the pre–Civil War period it had not been uncommon for presidents to provide a written explanation concerning their decision not to sign a particular bill, by the late nineteenth century and thereafter this practice had largely been abandoned. President Cleveland, for example, frequently wrote nothing on bills he had declined to sign, while President Harrison sometimes wrote "Let this bill die." The majority of bills pocket vetoed in this latter period most often have no comments from the president at all.

With the single exception of the incident in the House during the second session of the Sixty-Ninth Congress, Mitchell and Reeder "have been unable to find any case where either House of Congress has ever proceeded on the theory that a bill so pocketed had become a law." Further, "no such bill has ever been spread on the statute books, or afterwards recognized as law." Indeed, as Mitchell emphasized once again, "in a case like this, practical construction is controlling." To accept Lewis's argument "would be to resurrect 120 bills, pocketed, as was this one, at various dates since the adoption of the Constitution, and place them on the statute books." It is interesting that Mitchell did not find it necessary to say anything further concerning this graphic possibility he had mentioned in his brief. He probably assumed that such a possibility in no way would be acceptable to the Taft Court, and ultimately his confidence was not misplaced.

William Lewis had urged the Supreme Court to respect the lower court precedents upholding his arguments concerning the pocket veto, and William Mitchell acknowledged that there were a few state court decisions sustaining them. He discussed these findings in the final section of his brief. But for every favorable holding Lewis cited, Mitchell found another state decision reaching a contrary conclusion. What Lewis had argued, however, represented a major shift in constitutional law that would disregard more than a century of consistent legislative practice.

In two areas, Mitchell concluded that the state decisions did not justify such a step. They do not demonstrate, he argued, "such weight of authority in favor of the proposition that legislative rather than calendar days are meant in the provisions dealing with the return of unapproved bills as to cast doubt upon the long established practice respecting Federal legislation." Further, "in the State decisions there is no preponderance of opinion in favor of the position that a bill may be returned to officers of the legislature when the legislature itself is not in session." Both precedent and practice, therefore, "lead inevitably to the conclusion that the ad interim adjournment of Congress in this case prevented the return of the bill without Presidential approval, and that the Court of Claims was right in holding that it had not become a law."

* * *

Besides the briefs filed by William Lewis and William Mitchell, a third party asked the Supreme Court for leave to submit an amicus brief in the pocket veto case, one who will be familiar to the reader from his leading role in the House debate concerning the alleged legality of a bill that had been pocket vetoed by President Coolidge in 1926 and discussed in the previous chapter. In 1929, when he submitted his brief on behalf of the House Committee on the Judiciary, Hatton Sumners was in the midst of what would be a thirty-four-year tenure (seventeen consecutive terms) as a congressman representing Texas. In 1932 he would become the chair of the Judiciary Committee, a post he would retain until he retired from Congress in 1946. While his appearance in this case represented the first instance of his role as an amicus on behalf of his colleagues, it would later be followed by two more appearances in such a capacity before his tenure had concluded.

Sumners, who never graduated from law school, emphasized in his first paragraph that judicial determination of the questions in this case "is a matter of the greatest importance and concern . . . particularly to the House of Representatives who have . . . reached the conclusion that bills [such as S. 3185] have become law." The question becomes "important to the Congress since upon its determination depends whether such bills expire, necessitating their reintroduction and the expenditure of time and the delay incident to proceeding with them *de novo.*" By 1929 it might appear that the constitutionality of the pocket veto had been debated almost to excess. Already William Lewis had presented written arguments concerning this cause no fewer than three times. Of necessity, therefore, Sumners had to retrace and repeat many of the points Lewis had previously put forth. Yet the congressman approached the matter of the pocket veto in his own way, and with a style somewhat different from that of Lewis.

At the outset, Sumners observed that the framers "were conscious of the fact that they were assembling the greatest Constitution of all time, suitable for the Government of a great territory." Thus they were not "writing petty statutes." They did not trouble to specify, for example, how a bill was to be presented to the president, or how that official was to return it to the House or Senate. "The right of possession by the President of bills being temporary, and given for a definite specific purpose, any unnecessary retention of them" or "unnecessary detention of [a] bill made deliberately for the purpose of denying to the Congress an opportunity to [re]pass the bill is . . . a . . . usurpation of power." In short, as Sumners would repeatedly reiterate, except when implemented only after a final adjournment, the pocket veto was a blatant unconstitutional abuse of the presidential function.

Sumners pointed to the fact that when the veto process is in play, "every essential [legislative] step in this procedure shall be of record." Yet the president in using a pocket veto needed to document or explain nothing. His silence and inaction have the same power and effect as that of an absolute veto, an authority specifically rejected by the framers. They were, insisted the future chairman of the House Committee on the Judiciary, "not unmindful or negligent of the fact that it is not in keeping with the public interest that any individual, however high his station, should have the sole power by action or inaction to kill important legislation and hide his reasons therefor[e] under a blanket of secrecy. Every reasonable construction should be invoked to minimize such a possibility."

Sumners added that even with the veto that is authorized by the Constitution, "the President is commanded to put his reasons in writing, and the House to which the return is made is commanded to record those reasons, in their entirety, upon their permanent record books." Given the fact that by 1929 Sumners had served more than twenty years in Congress, and that in his brief he spoke for his committee colleagues, his emphasis on the inherent authority of the legislature is not surprising. To be sure, there will always be a number of unfinished bills at the end of a final session that "will die with the Congress whose bills they are." But that is a very different matter from a constitutional construction that permits "them to die short of the death of the Congress which originated them." Such is the impact of the pocket veto. "It is not conceivable that the framers of the Constitution incorporated any language susceptible of a construction which would arbitrarily make them die, unfinished, short of the point fixed by unavoidable necessity."

It has now become common, according to the Texas Democrat, after congressional adjournment or even a recess "for it to be published through the public press that a given bill, known to be disapproved by the President, is being held by him and would become the victim of the pocket veto." One should understand exactly what such a course of action implied.

> In such a case it would not be a failure of legislation by reason of lack of time on the part of the President to make up his mind, but a failure because the President had made up his mind; not a failure because the bill was returned as the Constitution directs and had not received the necessary two-thirds vote to overcome the President's objections, but a failure because the President, with his mind already made up in opposition to the bill, had taken advantage of a situation and for the purpose of depriving Congress of an opportunity to complete the discharge of their constitutional duty had delayed the discharge of his constitutional duty.

Indeed, the entire conception of the pocket veto "is at variance with the Constitution." Heretofore, according to Sumners, "with few exceptions Presidents have used this power with moderation, but experience has proven that this sort of power entrusted to an individual cannot be held in proper bounds by the maximum of restraint and virtue which human nature may be expected to supply." Now "we have reached the point at which the claim is actually made in this case and in this Court, that a single individual has the power in a given situation to do that which in effect amounts to an absolute veto of an act of the National Legislature, and to hold as a constitutional privilege his reasons and motives undisclosed, and that, too, with regard to matters of first magnitude." In truth, "the legislative department of the government is as much responsible as the Presidents for our having taken the wrong direction which brought us to our present condition."

Sumners might have been referring here to the fact that thus far, neither branch of Congress had undertaken any definitive action to challenge use of the pocket veto—all the more as it had been ongoing for more than a century. However, it is never too late to raise a challenge of unconstitutionality before the federal courts, and perhaps if William Lewis had not hesitated to turn the Okanogan case into the pocket veto litigation, the House might have acted on its own, instead of merely joining it as an amici. That Sumners may have been thinking along such an eventuality may be inferred from a couple of paragraphs lurking in the final pages of his brief.

He cautioned the justices that "to permit practices, especially practices originating out of a misconception of the Constitution [such as the pocket veto] to fasten erroneous interpretations upon our written Constitution . . . would be a fatal policy." For Sumners, "no generation or number of generations by a disregard of the plan of the Constitution or confusion as to it, can deprive those who come after them of the full benefit of its provisions." On the other hand, "the practical difficulty of inaugurating a reverse practice once it is recognized that a given practice has crystallized itself into a controlling constitutional construction warns with compelling persuasion against such a recognition." In short, what should be done with the pocket veto?

The worst thing that could be done is to do nothing. This option would assume that "in the construction of a written Constitution it never should be held that practice can effect that which practice cannot change." Such a consideration would weigh heavily against any suggestion implicit in Mitchell's brief "that the length of time during which the pocket veto has been practiced has a bearing upon [its] constitutionality." It does not. Endurance is not to be equated with legitimacy, and continuation should not be assumed to imply constitutionality. In fact, use of the pocket veto "and the inevitable strain upon the relationship of the President and Congress . . . makes this a question of major importance." Although Sumners avoided a direct statement to this effect, within his argument is his insistence that if the president can effectively kill a bill without explanation, truly the branches of the federal government are not co-equal.

In the final pages of his brief, the Texas Democrat re-echoed several of the points raised earlier by William S. Lewis in his brief to the court. As to the claim that the veto must be directed to a house of Congress only when in active session, "that conception is . . . a sort of fossil now which attached itself to our Constitution." It cannot now "be accepted that practices, under different conditions, can limit the liberty which the Constitution gives. Erroneous conceptions of [this document] however long held cannot affect the rights of those who follow in responsibility to discharge their duties as the Constitution itself allows." Further, Sumners emphasized that if the president could sign bills into law during an adjournment by Congress, there was no reason why he could not disapprove a measure as well.

The Constitution "does not fix any methods by which the President is to get the bill back. He can return it in person to the Clerk or Speaker, and send it by an agent, or if he wants to risk the bill becoming a law because not returned in time, he can send it by mail." What he may not do, however, is to "keep it in his pocket." With the clerk ready, willing, and able to receive the bill, "the President cannot kill [it]. The Constitution is its protector. He can burn the paper in his possession, but he cannot kill the bill. The President must get the bill back to the House of origin within ten days allowed or the Constitution makes it a law." Regardless of what "may be the conclusion as to the right to make constructive delivery, and regardless of all intervening questions when the ten days shall have expired[,] which marks the longest period of time under which construction is allowed and the bill has not been returned, it is a law." Such is true of the bill at issue in this case.

Using almost the identical language Lewis had employed in concluding his brief, now Sumners reiterated the point again. "Subsequent construction can never alter the text of the Constitution or enlarge or narrow its boundaries." Nor can precedents "in effect fasten themselves upon the Constitution to remain a perpetual hindrance and limitation upon future generations compelled to deal with ever-increasing responsibilities." Finally, he offered a few sentences concerning the justices of the high court. It is a "matter of the greatest importance . . . that the courts when called to the decision of a constitutional question deem it their duty to lead back those who have wandered however long or however far and direct them again into the ways of the Constitution." Such would indeed be appropriate in this case. The time may come, however, "when the reverse will be true; when instead of the Courts . . . guiding people and public officials back into the ways of the Constitution, by their opinions they establish barriers which prevent their return." His observations "are offered in opposition to what seems to have been the position of the Government in the Court below." When the Supreme Court handed down its decision in May 1929, Justice Sanford observed that Sumners "has aided us by a comprehensive and forcible presentation against the conclusions of the court below." How persuasive the justices found it turned out to be a very different matter.

Where did all this leave the pocket veto? Sumners found it laden with constitutional flaws in at least five instances:

(1) [The Constitution] imposes on the President the duty of returning a bill to which he objects, and secures to the Congress which originates it the benefit of his objections upon the second consideration of the bill. The pocket veto relieves the President of this duty and deprives the Congress of the reasons for the President's objections. (2) The Constitution demands that Congress shall enter the President's objections to legislation ... upon their journal. The pocket veto makes this impossible. (3) The Constitution requires that the President's objections be made known to the Congress and the country. The pocket veto violates this mandate. (4) The Constitution demands that Congress be afforded opportunity to reconsider and act upon the President's objections ... if they see fit to do so. The pocket veto denies them this opportunity. (5) Using the pocket veto gives to the President a power over legislation denied to him by the Constitutional Convention.

On March 11, William Lewis, William Mitchell, and Hatton Sumners summarized before the Supreme Court what they had detailed earlier in their written briefs. Sumners repeated the points he had raised in his conclusion and emphasized that the Constitution did not and does not give the president an absolute veto power. Using the pocket veto, however, "does give to the President an absolute veto." Mitchell stated that presidents had utilized the pocket veto since 1812, more than a century ago. Over a hundred such bills had been presumed to be dead as a result. Congress had never objected to the practice until 1927, when the House Judiciary Committee had adopted a resolution that S. 3185 had become a law. For the high court to rule against the pocket veto would resuscitate these 120 bills, which might—as Mitchell put it—"lead to serious consequences." Lewis insisted that the practice of the pocket veto "was an outgrowth of mistaken conceptions as to the nature of Congress and its sittings." The *New York Times* reported that "interest of the Court in this constitutional question" was reflected by questions raised from the justices, who "took the case under advisement." Two months passed with no word from the court.

CHAPTER 6

The Pocket Veto and the Supreme Court, 1929–1938

In 1929 the US Supreme Court had seen no change in membership since 1925. An all-white, all-male tribunal, as it had been from 1789 and would remain until 1967, the court consisted of seven Protestants, one Jew, and one Catholic. Its oldest member in terms of age, seniority, and distinction was Oliver Wendell Holmes, who had been appointed in 1902 by President Theodore Roosevelt. Holmes would serve as an associate justice for the next thirty years. A graduate of Harvard College and a twice-wounded veteran of the Civil War, he had been chief justice of the Massachusetts Supreme Judicial Court until Roosevelt brought him to Washington. By 1929 this jurist had become an icon of the American legal establishment. Indeed, he remained on the bench until after his ninetieth birthday, producing more than his share of written decisions on behalf of his brethren.

On the eve of oral arguments for the pocket veto case, the average age for the justices was sixty-nine, with Holmes approaching ninety and Harlan F. Stone the youngest at fifty-seven. Two distinct blocs within the court could be identified. Prior to the court's weekly conference, Chief Justice William Howard Taft had taken to convening what might be described as an informal cadre of hard-core conservatives. It consisted of himself, Willis Van Devanter, George Sutherland, James McReynolds, and Pierce Butler, occasionally joined by Edward Sanford. For his part, and also on a regular basis, Louis Brandeis would host the more liberal remaining court members, including himself, Holmes, and Stone. Although no type of court alignment should be described as permanent, by 1929 this division could be considered well established. With the exceptions of Holmes and Brandeis who had attained national stature, as a whole the Taft Court was not a distinguished body of jurists.

Paraphrasing a remark about Taft attributed to Brandeis, perhaps it can be said that they represented a "first rate–second rate" tribunal.

Known as "Primus inter Pares" (first among equals), but in fact less distinguished by far as a jurist than either Holmes or Louis Brandeis, was the chief justice, William Howard Taft. No member of the high court either before or since has brought to the bench such a varied résumé as he possessed: Ohio Superior Court judge, solicitor general of the United States, circuit judge, governor-general of the Philippines, secretary of war, president of the United States, professor of law at Yale University, and chief justice of the Supreme Court. As president from 1909 to March 1913, Taft had appointed five new members of the Supreme Court and elevated a current member, Edward White, to become chief justice in 1911. Although Taft had yearned to be chief justice since his law school days, he harbored little hope that such could ever become a reality. In 1921, however, two events occurred: in March, a Republican, Warren Harding, became president, and in May, Chief Justice White passed away. After pulling every possible string that he could, and after a number of weeks replete with anxious waiting, in June Taft received his wish. Harding did indeed name the first and thus far only former president to the court. The Senate did not even bother to refer his name to the Judiciary Committee but confirmed him on the same day it received his nomination.

In May 1929 Taft was in the midst of what would be his final year of life. By 1928 he was in failing health, and one year later this trend had been exacerbated. During the early years of his tenure, from 1921 to 1925, the chief justice demonstrated impressive mastery of his court. But toward the end, his leadership qualities had ebbed, with dissents now notable for their frequency. Worried that the "Bolsheviki" (Taft's term for Brandeis, Holmes, and Stone) might be able somehow to cobble a majority on the court, he had cultivated a core of conservative jurists, Van Devanter, McReynolds, Sutherland, and Pierce Butler, a group with whom Taft often voted, as did Edward Sanford, the justice who had been selected by Taft to write the opinion in the pocket veto case. Thus, the Taft majority for the most part stood at least at five and usually six. With Holmes close to his ninetieth birthday and Brandeis already seventy-three, "we can probably solve everything if we can only live, because delay makes for conservatism." Taft insisted he must stay on the court "to prevent the Bolsheviki from getting control."

Indeed, an aura of judicial conservatism had enveloped the Taft Court from the very beginning. At least four of its specific characteristics might be noted here. They included a strong emphasis on the rights of property; a deep attachment to liberty of contract; a distrust of regulatory legislation, especially by the state; and repeated emphasis on the limited powers of the judiciary even as the decisions of his court augmented it. Taken together they can be labeled as "classical legal thought." Although Taft did not live to see its decline, after 1938 classical legal thought appeared to have been derailed by the New Deal Express, with Franklin Delano Roosevelt as its engineer. By the time of his third reelection in 1944, Roosevelt had remade the Taft Court.

In 1929, however, it remained wrapped in the mantle of classical legal thought. Next to Holmes was Willis Van Devanter. Selected for the Eighth Circuit Court of Appeals by Theodore Roosevelt in 1903, "Van" had been Taft's third appointment to the high court in 1910. Albeit only on rare occasions, sometimes he displayed a tinge of progressive thought, for example, upholding the Federal Employee Liability Act and affirming an almost open-ended congressional investigatory authority. Among the Taft Court justices, Van Devanter seems to have had the most difficulty in producing his written decisions, even as his skill in shaping the court's findings determined in the weekly conferences was apparently unequaled.

Ironically enough, the same president—Woodrow Wilson—probably appointed both the worst and one of the truly distinguished members of the Taft Court. Indeed, James McReynolds has the dubious distinction of being the most obnoxious justice ever to serve on the high court. A graduate from Vanderbilt University, and argumentative, aloof, abrasive, and bigoted, he was well described by Taft as "selfish to the last degree . . . fuller of prejudice than any man I have known, and one who seems to delight in making others uncomfortable." About the only field of federal regulation that he found acceptable was antitrust legislation. Monopolies were "essentially wicked," and enforcing the Sherman Act was "a moral obligation." For the most part, however, McReynolds opposed both state and federal authority. Woodrow Wilson found McReynolds, who had been appointed his attorney general, to be a disruptive presence in the cabinet. In 1914 Wilson placed McReynolds on the Supreme Court, where he well deserved the description by his former clerk as "all in all the most contemptible and mediocre old man I ever came into contact with. His selfishness and vindictiveness are unbelievable."

In spite of the McReynolds legacy (he lived until 1946), Woodrow Wilson deserves great credit for placing one of the most outstanding figures in our legal history on the Supreme Court. Like McReynolds, Louis Brandeis had been born in Kentucky. But there all similarity ended. He never attended college, and after several years of travel and study in Europe, he was considered bright enough to enter Harvard Law School, from which he graduated in 1877. As a law student, Brandeis appears to have set a record for academic distinction apparently unequaled either in his lifetime or thereafter. As a very successful lawyer, by 1916 Brandeis had become known as "the people's attorney," possibly a reference to the fact that he took on and prevailed in a number of cases that he considered to concern the public interest, and without fee. Together with his close friend Justice Holmes, on the Taft Court Brandeis sought—often in vain—to shape a progressive, living law.

Besides the Taft appointment in 1921, it fell to President Harding to make three more selections to the court. In September 1922 he nominated former Utah senator George Sutherland, a close friend as well as an old acquaintance of the new chief justice. By October 2 he had been unanimously confirmed by the Senate, taken the oaths of office, and seated on the bench. Although very much a legal classicalist in thought, Sutherland was not quite in the reactionary mode of McReynolds. Nevertheless, Brandeis was "much disappointed in Sutherland. He is a mediocre Taft." The chief justice, on the other hand, considered Van Devanter and Sutherland among his closest associates on the court.

While Taft had nothing to do with Sutherland's appointment or confirmation, the same cannot be said for Harding's final choices as justices. Very familiar with Harding's attorney general, Harry Daugherty—a notorious Ohio political hack—Taft had not hesitated to put himself at Daugherty's service as an advisor on possible judicial nominees. Well aware of his own notoriety as a Ohio Republican operative, Daugherty was prompt to accept Taft's offer. Although the chief justice was quick to downplay any claims to influence with either Harding or his attorney general, the truth appears to have been more prosaic. If Taft by no means controlled the nominating process, "it did mean that if he objected to a particular candidate, that candidate had practically no chance of nomination."

Harding's next appointment to the high court—that of Minnesotan Pierce Butler, a devout Catholic, self-taught attorney, and very conservative Democrat—can be attributed in great measure to the complex but ultimately successful tactics employed by Taft to bring about the nomination. With only two Democrats on the current court (McReynolds and Brandeis), Taft had looked around for a Democrat "of sound views," in other words, more liberal than McReynolds but more conservative than Brandeis. The fact that a Catholic lawyer from Minnesota—well known to both Van Devanter and Taft—was available for the nomination resulted in Butler being the right man with the right credentials affiliated with the right party at the right time. With probable understatement, Taft later recalled, "I recommended him as well as I could to the President, and I think perhaps that had some influence."

Harding's final Supreme Court nominee came from the Federal District Court in Tennessee. An old friend of Taft, Edward Sanford had graduated from the University of Tennessee at the age of eighteen with two degrees, had gone on to Harvard for a third, and then to Harvard Law School where he received two more, and he was one of the founding editors of the *Harvard Law Review*. As a federal jurist, Sanford had supported both the League of Nations and the Versailles Treaty, two causes also dear to the chief justice. Taft wrote to his daughter in January 1923 that "Sanford's appointment would be entirely satisfactory. He is a charming man." Sanford would serve on the court for seven years, and he died on the same day as Taft, March 8, 1930. On a bench composed more of mediocre justices, albeit with three exceptions—Holmes, Brandeis, and Stone—Sanford does not stand out. He is of importance here, however, because he wrote the opinion for the court in the pocket veto case.

The unusual relationship between Harding, Daugherty, and the chief justice ended with Harding's sudden death in August 1923. To be sure, Harding had made four selections to the court, while his successor, Calvin Coolidge, himself a lawyer, had only one. Moreover, Coolidge did not demonstrate the insecurity and hesitation displayed by his predecessor in judicial appointments. He forced Harry Daugherty from his cabinet in the wake of the scandals within the late president's administration, in particular the Justice Department. To replace him, Coolidge chose his old friend and college classmate Harlan Fiske Stone, recently resigned as dean of the Columbia University Law School. In 1925 Coolidge had what in fact would be his only opportunity to select a high court nominee, and again he turned to Stone.

Taft claimed that "we are greatly rejoiced in this." The Stone appointment "was one eminently fit to be made." To his daughter Taft commented about Stone, "I like him. He is a straight-forward, honest, kindly, judicially tempered man." In January 1925 he wrote to Stone that "we are all most anxious to have you as a colleague." But these sentiments turned out to be fleeting. By 1929 he had recanted, and Taft's enthusiasm for Stone waned, all the more as Stone gravitated to the views held by Holmes and Brandeis. In 1929, with only a matter of months remaining in his life, Taft wrote of Stone that "his judgments I do not altogether consider safe." Even worse, "he definitely has ranged himself with Brandeis and with Holmes in a good many of our constitutional differences." The possibility that now President Herbert Hoover might appoint Stone as Taft's replacement filled the ailing chief justice with dread. For Hoover, such a move "would be a great mistake, for the reason that Stone is not a leader." Although Stone's later tenure as chief justice from 1941 to 1946 is beyond the scope of this study, it may be noted that Taft was prescient in his assessment.

These, then, were the nine justices who composed the Taft Court in May 1929, as it prepared to hand down the decision in the pocket veto case. Although it involved an important issue of constitutional law, Taft assigned the decision to a jurist who, while widely respected as a likeable colleague, was not regarded as a distinguished justice. According to Brandeis, Sanford "ought never to have been above [the district court]— a dull bourgeois mind—terribly tiresome." Indeed, "he is nice—but no spark of greatness; thoroughly bourgeois." His "mind gives one blurs; it does not clearly register." On May 27 Sanford delivered his opinion for a unanimous court. It now became possible to ascertain how influential and persuasive Lewis, Mitchell, and Sumners had been in their arguments to the justices.

* * *

Sanford began his opinion with the expected summary of the basic facts in this case, with which the reader will be well familiar. He also acknowledged the contribution of Hatton Sumners as amicus, observing that the Texas congressman "has aided us by a comprehensive and forcible presentation of arguments against the conclusion" of the Court of Claims. How much Sumners had actually "aided us," however, is open to question. In fact, Sanford went on to reject out of hand every major argument that the amicus had raised. Further, he distilled the extensive points presented by Lewis down to three.

In the first place, Lewis insisted that the only type of adjournment that prevents the president from returning a bill "is the final adjournment of the Congress. Since such an act terminates its existence, thus there is no legislative body to whom the bill can be returned for consideration." Moreover, an adjournment of the first session would not prevent the president from such a return "since the legislative existence of the Congress is not terminated." Nothing barred the chief executive from returning the bill to a secretary, clerk, or other appropriate agent of that house, to be held by him until Congress resumed its sitting at the next session. Finally, Lewis proposed that the "ten days" allowed for return of the bill as stated in the constitutional provision could be construed as meaning "legislative days," or days on which the Congress is in legislative session, rather than "calendar days," Sundays excepted.

With similar efficiency, Sanford reduced the arguments on behalf of the United States to one short paragraph, with four key points: (1) the term "adjournment" includes an interim adjournment such as the end of the first congressional session; (2) ten days could only mean ten calendar days; (3) the president could only return a bill to its house of origin when that body was in session; and (4) if that house is not in session it cannot be returned, and thus the president is prevented from acting within the prescribed time mandated by the Constitution. "This view," added Justice Sanford, "is supported by the practical construction given to the constitutional provision by the president through a long course of years, in which Congress has acquiesced." Here, Sanford borrowed almost literally from Mitchell's argument, and its inclusion offered a clear hint to the alert reader that the government's position would be sustained by the court, as indeed it was.

While Lewis and to a lesser extent Sumners had drawn on various state court decisions that, they claimed, supported their position, William Mitchell had insisted that the lack of uniformity in these various state court holdings rendered them of dubious value as precedents. Again Sanford borrowed from Mitchell's brief. He observed that examination of these state court holdings "discloses such a conflict of opinion . . . that, viewed as a whole, they furnish no substantial aid in the determination of the question here presented, and a detailed consideration of them here would not be helpful."

All the attorneys arguing this case agreed that the key constitutional section at issue concerned "the provision as to the return of a bill within a specified period of time," it being ten days, with Sundays excepted. Lewis and Sumners urged the high court to construe this section "in a manner that will give effect to the reciprocal rights and duties of the President and of Congress." Such a construction "would not enable [the president] to defeat a bill of which he disapproves by a silent and absolute veto, that is, a so-called pocket veto, which neither discloses his objections nor gives Congress an opportunity to pass the bill over them." Speaking for all his brethren, Sanford held first that Lewis and Sumners argued from "a misconception . . . of the situation resulting from an adjournment of Congress which prevents the President from returning the bill with his objections within the specified time."

In this context, Sanford added, use of the term "pocket veto" "does not accurately describe the situation, and is misleading in its implications in that it suggests that the failure of the bill in such a situation is necessarily due to the disapproval of the president and the intentional withholding of the bill from reconsideration." On the contrary, it is the adjournment of Congress that prevents the chief executive from returning the bill. Congress chooses when to adjourn, and if such action—taken within the ten-day limit—bars the president from fulfilling his required mandate, this "cannot properly be ascribed to the disapproval of the President . . . but is attributable solely to the action of Congress in adjourning." In other words, Sanford claimed that Congress, by rendering it impossible for the president to return a bill within the ten-day limit, in effect makes a pocket veto inevitable. Sanford cited an 1899 decision to the effect that if by adjournment Congress prevents the president from being able to return the bill within the required time limit, "then the bill fails and does not become a law" (175 U.S. 423).

Turning to his second finding, Sanford readily dismissed the contention raised by William Lewis that ten days "may be construed as meaning not calendar days, but 'legislative days,' that is, days during which Congress is in legislative session." The jurist wrote, "The words used in the Constitution are to be taken in their natural and obvious sense, and are to be given the meaning they have in common use unless there are very strong reasons to the contrary." In this case, he could find none. The "word 'days' means in ordinary and common usage calendar days." Further, "there is nothing whatever to justify changing this meaning" by inserting the word "legislative." No president or Congress "has ever suggested that the President has ten 'legislative days'. . . or proceeded upon that theory."

"Nor can we agree," Sanford added, with Lewis's argument that the "word 'adjournment' as used in the constitutional provision refers only to the final adjournment of the Congress." In the document itself, the word "adjournment" is not qualified by the word "final," "and there is nothing in the context which warrants the insertion of such a limitation." Sanford cited several instances in the document demonstrating that "the word is not limited to a final adjournment." Two of the three points insisted on by Lewis had now been rejected by the Court. The remaining issue was whether or not the bill in question "may be returned to the House, although not in session, by delivering it to an officer or agent of the House, to be held by him and delivered to the House when it resumes its sittings at the next session." Although both Lewis and Sumners had vigorously pushed this point, again Sanford dismissed it.

"We think that the House to which the bill is to be returned" must of necessity be a "House in session," that is, with "a quorum of the membership, a majority, one half and one more" present. The bill must be returned to the house when sitting in an organized capacity for the transaction of business. "No return can be made to the House when it is not in session as a collective body and its members are dispersed." Although at this point, Sanford had rejected the Lewis-Sumners argument by implication, he went on to deal with it directly.

"We find no substantial basis for the suggestion that although the House . . . is not in session the bill may nevertheless be returned . . . by delivering it . . . to an officer or agent of the House." In spite of the eloquence with which both Lewis and Sumners had pushed this point, he identified a number of constitutional deficiencies with it. A preliminary objection was quickly disposed of. "Aside from the fact that Congress has never enacted any such statute permitting such action," in addition, there is "no rule to that effect in either House." Indeed, even if Congress had authorized it, such a delivery "would not comply with the constitutional mandate," in at least three instances.

In the first place, the house not being in session could not have received the bill. Nor could it have entered the president's objections into its journal. Nor, finally, could it have proceeded to reconsider the bill. All of these steps are required by the Constitution. Moreover, "there is nothing in the Constitution which authorizes either House to make a nunc pro tunc [now for then] record of the return of a bill as of a date on which it had not, in fact, been returned." It had never been intended, Sanford insisted, that after an adjournment the president could deliver his objections to the bill "to some individual who should hold it in his hands for days, weeks or perhaps months . . . keeping the bill in . . . a state of suspended animation until the House resumes its sittings." Such was not a "timely" return of the bill, "which should not only be a matter of official record . . . but should enable Congress to proceed immediately with its reconsideration; and that the return of the bill should be an actual and public return to the House itself." There was no suggestion in existing federal law that the president could return a bill "to the Speaker, or Clerk, or any officer of the House; but the return must be made to the House as an organized body."

Sanford stated further that only one attempt had been made in Congress to "authorize the President to return a bill when the House in which it originated was not in session; and that this failed." Such a measure had been reported out by the Senate Judiciary Committee in 1868, and although it passed the Senate by a majority vote, "it was never reported from the Judiciary Committee of the House . . . and thus failed to pass the Congress. It does not appear that this suggestion has ever been renewed in Congress." For him, the absence of such interest was telling. "The views which we have expressed . . . are confirmed by the practical construction that has been given to it by the Presidents through a long course of years, in which Congress has acquiesced. Long settled and established practice is a consideration of great weight in a proper interpretation of constitutional provisions of this character." To the contrary,

Lewis and Sumners had essentially argued that if the basic constitutional premise is incorrect, it matters not how long its precedent has been followed.

Finally, Sanford turned to the Reeder report on the pocket veto, which had been transmitted by Calvin Coolidge to Congress in December 1928, and "the accuracy of which is not questioned." It cited and identified more than four hundred bills and resolutions that "were passed by Congress and submitted to the President less than ten days before a final or interim adjournment of Congress, which were not signed by the President nor returned with his disapproval." At least a hundred of them were instances in which the adjournment was that at the end of a session of Congress, to be distinguished from the final adjournment of the Congress, as was the case in 1926. "It does not appear that in any of these instances either House of Congress in any official manner questioned the validity and effect of the President's action in not returning the bill after the adjournment of the session, or proceeded on the theory that it had become a law . . . until the action was taken by the House Committee of the Whole in 1927." Without bothering to analyze these 119 measures in any detail,

> we think they show that for a long series of years . . . all the Presidents who have had occasion to deal with this question have adopted and carried into effect the construction of the constitutional provision that they were prevented from returning the bill . . . by the adjournment of the session of Congress; and that this construction has been acquiesced in by both Houses of Congress until 1927.

It followed, then, Sanford concluded, that when Congress adjourned on July 3, 1926, such action prevented Coolidge from returning S. 3185 within the ten-day limit. Because he could not return it, Congress could not reconsider the measure. Thus it had not become a law. Although Sanford acknowledged the forcefulness of Hatton Sumners's amicus brief, it had failed to persuade the court. So too had William Lewis been unsuccessful in his arguments. It was essential, according to Justice Brandeis, that a controversial point in constitutional law should be settled. Indeed, it was more important that it receive a definitive judicial resolution, rather than the issue at hand be settled "correctly." With the weight with more than a century of consistent legislative and executive interpretation of the pocket veto, in 1929 the Taft Court saw no reason to change it. In constitutional law, however, *nothing* is permanent except change. The pocket veto decision would last for less than a decade before undergoing significant judicial alteration.

* * *

In 1938 the high court returned to this topic once again when it announced the holding in *Wright v. United States* (302 U.S. 583). Of the nine justices who had cast the unanimous vote in 1929, five still sat on the bench, but one of them—George Sutherland—retired on January 17, 1938, the day *Wright* was handed down. Justices Brandeis, Butler, McReynolds, and Stone were all that remained of the Taft Court. They were joined by the three justices selected by Herbert Hoover: Chief Justice Charles Evans Hughes, Owen J. Roberts, and Benjamin Cardozo. By 1938 Franklin Roosevelt had made his first selection from among the eight newcomers whom he would ultimately appoint to the Supreme Court, Alabama Democratic senator Hugo Black. Seriously ill, Justice Cardozo did not participate in the final deliberations and vote. Thus eight justices ruled in the *Wright* case.

At first glance, it might appear that these two cases were very similar. Both had involved successful efforts to gain congressional passage of a special bill, authorizing the Court of Claims to hear and adjudicate plaintiffs' claims. Both plaintiffs had assumed that—in the apparent absence of a presidential veto within the days stipulated in the Constitution—their respective bills had become laws. Both had filed suit in the Court of Claims only to have the United States respond that neither bill had become a federal statute. Finally, both had been rebuffed by this court. Despite these similarities, there were significant differences between the 1929 and 1938 decisions, and the latter resulted in major modifications of the earlier unanimous opinion.

The *Wright* case has a complicated history. In 1918 a Chicago-based manufacturer, David Wright, alleged that he spent more than $92,000 to refurbish and rehabilitate a plant so it could manufacture heavy-duty lathes for ongoing use by the Ordinance Department of the US Army. He received one contract for $20,000, but the November armistice ended the possibility of further agreements. Alleging further that he had relied on the good faith of two army representatives who had assured him that further contracts would be forthcoming, after the armistice Wright sued in the Court of Claims, seeking a minimal payment for the $92,000. He did not prevail, as that court ruled that whomever he dealt with in the military "had no authority to contract on behalf of, or so to bind the Government."

But David Wright persisted. Indeed, he appears to have been a resourceful character. Somehow he managed to gain congressional approval for a second opportunity before the Court of Claims, giving it the opportunity to "reinstate, reopen, and rehear" Wright's case, to "readjudicate the same and determine the costs or expenditures he may have incurred" in the rehabilitation of his manufacturing plant. By the spring of 1936 this bill had passed both houses, and on April 24 it had been presented to President Franklin D. Roosevelt. Apart from these apparent similarities between the 1929 pocket veto case and *Wright v. United States*, significant differences can be identified.

The first difference to be noted is that in the pocket veto case, there is no doubt that both houses of Congress had adjourned for a period of about five months, with this action marking the end of the first session of the particular Congress involved. Such was not the case with *Wright*. The bill in question—which originated in the Senate—had indeed passed both houses and had been received by the president on April 24, 1936. The ten-day period for his consideration in accord with the Constitution ended on May 6. Meanwhile, the Senate recessed from May 4 until May 7, while the House remained in session. When President Roosevelt returned the unsigned bill and his veto message to the Senate on May 5 (still within the requisite time frame), that body was not in session to receive it. Therefore, Roosevelt's messenger delivered both the unsigned bill and his written objections to the secretary of the Senate. When the Senate reconvened two days later, the presidential message was read to the senators, and without debate or discussion the bill was referred to the Senate Committee on Claims. No further action concerning it appears to have been taken either by the Senate or the president.

After an interval of almost four months, on September 14, David Wright filed his petition with the Court of Claims and was met with an objection by the United States that the bill had never become a law. The Court of Claims sustained the objection and dismissed Wright's petition without formal opinion. Hence Wright sought a writ of certiorari from the high court. Wright's counsel urged the justices to grant the writ for several reasons. In the first place, the fact structure in *Wright* raised a question that had never been decided by the court: does a bill become a law "without the President's signature when he is not prevented from returning it" because Congress had adjourned, with the House still in session, but because the Senate—in which the bill had originated—had taken a three-day recess? Such is precisely what happened in this case, and this question needed to be resolved by the justices.

Moreover, counsel insisted that the Court of Claims had erred in dismissing Wright's petition because "it is only in case the President is prevented by an adjournment of the Congress from returning the bill that it does not become a law, and not [as happened here] in case the President may be prevented by an adjournment or recess of one House of Congress." Finally, counsel claimed that the Court of Claims holding conflicted with the pocket veto decision of 1929. That decision had held that the bill must be returned to the appropriate house while in *active session*, "and thus a delivery to the Secretary of the Senate, as in this case . . . does not fulfill the constitutional requirement." Ashby Williams expanded on these points in his argument accompanying the petition for certiorari.

Counsel listed several "errors" by the Court of Claims. It had failed to recognize that as the Congress had NOT adjourned, with the House still in session, nothing had prevented the president from returning the bill, and therefore it had become law without his signature. Further, the "return" by the president to the secretary of the Senate was in fact not a return as mandated by the Constitution. Finally, only an adjournment by *both* houses of Congress within the ten-day limitation renders a return by the president impossible, with the bill not becoming a law. Such was not the case in this litigation, and thus the Senate bill in question, S. 713, had in fact become a law, as a pocket veto was impossible. Nowhere in the Constitution, added Williams, did the framers "provide that when one House of Congress, by its adjournment, prevented the return of a Bill should it fail to become a law."

Unlike the pocket veto case, where the United States had joined William S. Lewis in seeking a writ of certiorari, in 1937 the solicitor general not only declined to support the motion but also submitted a brief in opposition to it. Stanley Reed, for whom in a matter of months the future held appointment to the very court before which he argued, presented a brief that came to less than half the length of Williams's argument. Moreover, he questioned plaintiff's reliance on the pocket veto decision. Reed quoted Justice Sanford's assertion that "since the President may return a bill at any time within the allotted period, he is prevented from returning it . . . if, by reason of the adjournment it is impossible for him to return it to the House in which it originated on the last day of that period." Here, because the return of the Senate bill had been prevented by the action of the Senate, "it automatically failed to become a law in the absence of the President's signature."

Reed concluded that in this case, "there exists no conflict" with the Court of Claims holding. As was true in 1928, so it was true almost a decade later. While the government saw no necessity for issuance of the writ, if the court saw fit to grant it, which the justices did, still the Court of Claims holding should be affirmed. Williams had argued that since the "return" to the secretary of the Senate was not in accord with the Constitution, the Senate bill had become law, as it were, by default. The pocket veto had not been and could not be exercised. In opposition, the solicitor general took the position that because the president had been unable to return the bill to the Senate, due to a temporary adjournment, automatically it had failed to become a law. With the decision to grant certiorari, both sides had yet another opportunity to submit written arguments to the court. This time, counsel went into greater detail concerning their respective claims.

Williams reiterated once again that the delivery of the bill and FDR's objections to the secretary of the Senate did not make a return as was in fact required by the Constitution. Further, Williams insisted that the term "Congress" could only apply to both the House and the Senate. There is no way, then, that FDR's messenger had returned the bill to Congress. The adjournment mentioned in the provision is rather the adjournment of both House and Senate, representing the whole and complete legislative power of the United States. It is only when this Congress has adjourned and thus prevented the return of a bill not approved or signed by the president that it fails to become a law, such being the pocket veto.

Williams next questioned whether in fact the three-day recess of the Senate from May 4 to May 7 had actually "prevented the return of the bill" in this case. Roosevelt had received it on April 24, and the Senate recessed on May 4. According to counsel, Roosevelt had been in possession of the bill for "8 full weekdays ... and 2 Sundays. ... This was a longer time than the average time that all Presidents have held such bills." Further, he stated that thirty-nine out of fifty-five framers had been members of the Continental Congress and were well aware that "legislative bodies frequently take a temporary recess for a day or two." Yet they provided that only when the Congress by their adjournment prevented a return of a bill should it fail to become law, and nowhere did they mandate that "when one House ... by its adjournment, prevented the return of a bill, should it fail to become a law."

Williams proceeded to state explicitly what he had intimated in this assertion. Since all legislative powers granted by the Constitution are vested in the Congress, "it must be inferred that any bill which has passed the Congress and been presented to the President is a law, unless it affirmatively appears that something subsequent to such presentation ... has intervened to prevent its becoming a law, and the only thing, under the express language, that can happen is the open and notorious [known?] adjournment of the Congress." But such had not occurred in the context of this case, and the veto power "being in derogation of the legislative power, the extent and manner of its exercise must be controlled by the express language of the Constitution." If this be done, S. 713 became a law because of FDR's inaction, until it was too late for him to take action.

The only possible way in which it can be held that this bill failed to become a law, insisted Williams, "is to write into the Constitution something which is not there. ... To hold that S. 713 did not become a law means changing the words [from] 'unless the Congress by their adjournment prevent its return,' to read 'unless the Congress or the House in which it shall have originated by their adjournment prevents its return.' This ... cannot possibly be done without absolutely destroying every fundamental concept of constitutional interpretation." S. 713 "has never been returned to the Senate." Thus, "at the expiration of the constitutional 10 days [its] status became fixed by the Constitution and no subsequent action by either the President or Congress could change that status." Because Congress had not adjourned, a pocket veto was impossible. Hence the bill became a law "by reason of the President's failure to constitutionally return it."

Finally, Williams reminded the justices that the object of constitutional construction "is to give effect to the intent of its framers. . . . This intent is to be found in the instrument itself, and when the text of a constitutional provision is not ambiguous the courts, in giving construction thereto, are not at liberty to search for its meaning beyond the instrument." The clear language of the veto clause in the context of this case required that Wright should prevail.

*　*　*

Counsel for the United States began his reply to the Williams argument by subdividing the essential question raised in this litigation into two distinct queries: (1) Does a bill become a law without the president's signature where ten days after receiving it he is prevented from returning the bill to the house wherein it originated "because that House has adjourned"? (2) Does a bill become a law without the president's signature when on the ninth day after it was presented to him, he "returns the bill together with his objections to the Secretary of the Senate . . . the Senate being then in recess pursuant to an adjournment for three days"? Both parties agreed that when the Senate reconvened, the secretary had informed that body of the president's action, whereupon both his message and the bill were referred to the Senate Committee on Claims and "no further action was taken thereafter." Under these conditions, Sam Whitaker argued that from the outset S. 713 had never become a law, a position supported by the Court of Claims.

The attorney for the government emphasized that at least in "every other situation than the one presented here," it has been assumed that the president had ten days in which to indicate his approval or rejection of measures presented to him by the Congress. In this case, however, one house of Congress had adjourned at the end of seven days, while the other house remained in session. How does such a step affect the ten-day rule just mentioned? According to Wright's attorney, adjournment by a single house in effect "reduced from ten to seven days the time in which the President's veto power can be exercised." But such a result, according to the pocket veto case, is unconstitutional. Ten days means just that, not seven days. Further, added the government's counsel, when an adjournment prevents a return of a bill, "that adjournment is equally one of the Congress . . . whether it be an adjournment of both Houses acting concurrently, an adjournment of one House acting with the consent of the other, or an adjournment of a single House acting alone." According to the 1936 calendar, the period from April 24 to the day of Senate adjournment includes eight days. Therefore, it would appear that FDR had every right to return the bill when he did. Indeed, the assistant attorney general insisted that the

> powers of the executive and legislative branches . . . were intended to function harmoniously. To carve out an exception to the [long] established doctrine protecting the President's power of veto from destruction or impairment by Congress would be to deny accepted canons of constitutional interpretation and to subtract much of the meaning from this Court's express declarations concerning the scope of the power.

Thus the Court had previously held that the president could approve a bill during a short recess taken by Congress, notwithstanding the fact that one of the houses had adjourned. The justices had also held that he could approve a bill after final adjournment by Congress. This case, however, concerned not approval but rather presidential disapproval of a measure and his unsuccessful attempt to return it to the house of origin, which had adjourned, while the other house remained in session.

Counsel for Wright had insisted that "the power of the President to disapprove a bill at any time during the ten-day period is dependent upon the willingness of the originating House to remain in session." By choosing to adjourn for three days, in effect the Senate had reduced the president's window of opportunity to seven days, in spite of the constitutional mandate that it is to be ten. Here the attorney for the government resorted to the well-established legalistic, slippery slope argument. If, as happened in this case, the House chose to reduce the period to seven days, "no reason appears why it may not by successive adjournments, commencing on the day the bill is presented . . . destroy the opportunity altogether. . . . Indeed, if it is the fact of session by the other House which is decisive, the argument goes to the extent of permitting the originating House to adjourn with the consent of the other for the entire period and so to prevent any exercise of the veto power whatever." Yet this court had previously held that "the [veto] power thus conferred cannot be narrowed or cut down by Congress, nor the time within which it is to be exercised lessened, directly or indirectly."

Counsel for the plaintiff had explained that there are two methods by which the chief executive "may make effective his disapproval of a bill." First, he can return it with his objections to the house from which it originated. Second, where the Congress has adjourned, thus preventing its return, the president simply ignores the bill and does not sign it. This, of course, is the traditional pocket veto. In this case, plaintiffs claimed that neither option was available to the president. He could not return the bill to the Senate as it had adjourned. Further, Congress had not prevented its return, as mandated. Rather, it was the Senate's action. Thus by default, he insisted, the bill became a law because neither of the two methods for utilizing the veto could be exercised.

The government's attorney rejected this contention out of hand, as "contrary to the plain intendment [*sic*] of the Constitution." Moreover, with the exception of the plaintiff, there was minimal legal support for the argument. "So far was the practice in this case from being established in the petitioner's favor, that it was assumed both by Congress and the President to be the contrary. The Senate, when the President's disapproval was communicated to it, took no cognizance thereof and referred the bill to the Claims Committee," where it died on final adjournment of the Congress. "No further action had been taken, and the bill was never treated as having become a law." Finally, it mattered not "what Congress and the President thought, but what the Constitution provides." That document simply "does not contemplate that the President's power of veto can be curtailed, or the opportunity for deliberation in advance of its exercise cut short in such fashion as the contention of the petitioner would permit." As had been true in 1929, so again in 1938 counsel for the government asked that the judgment of the Court of Claims be affirmed.

* * *

Lawyers argued the *Wright* case on November 16, 1937. Considering that the Thanksgiving recess and the holiday season both followed, it is not surprising that the decision was not announced until January 17, 1938. On the other hand, given these external factors, it does not appear that the court spent a great deal of time on this case. Eight justices voted on the outcome, and Chief Justice Hughes announced the decision for six of them. Justice Stone, joined by Brandeis, concurred with the result, but not with the chief justice's opinion. In a confusing judgment, all eight justices agreed that S. 713 had not become a law. Beyond that, unanimity faded.

At the outset, the chief justice turned to the question of "whether 'the Congress by their adjournment' prevented the return of the bill by the President within" the ten days granted him. If so, as a matter of course the provision for a pocket veto would apply. But Hughes had no difficulty summarily rejecting the premise implicit in the question. Congress, he stated outright, had not adjourned. Only the Senate was in recess, and that for a period of three days. The Constitution defined the Congress as "a Senate and a House of Representatives." Whenever the document uses the word "Congress," it manifestly refers to "the entire legislative body consisting of both Houses. Nowhere in the Constitution are the words 'the Congress' used to describe a single House." Indeed, the constitutional language "is entirely free from ambiguity, and there is no occasion for construction."

Hughes conceded that an alternative view that a bill could not be returned by the president to the originating house "when that House during the session of Congress is in recess" had been suggested, "but we think that the premise is faulty." Plainly, he added, the taking of a three-day recess "is not an adjournment by the Congress. The Session of Congress continues." At which point, Hughes veered away from the 1928 pocket veto analysis. He stated that in FDR's return of the bill to the secretary of the Senate, "there was no violation of any express requirement of the Constitution," if only because that document "does not define what shall constitute a return of a bill or deny the use of appropriate agencies in effecting the return."

Nor, continued the chief justice, did the fact that one house was in recess make any difference. The organization of the Senate continued "and was intact." Indeed, the secretary of the Senate "was able to receive, and did receive the bill." All parties were familiar with the process of presenting a bill to the president by messenger,

> and why may it not be received [from him] by the accredited agent
> of the legislative body? To say that the President cannot return a bill

when the House in which it originated is in recess during the session of Congress, and thus affords an opportunity for the passing of the bill over the President's objections, is to ignore the plainest practical consideration and by implying a requirement of an artificial formality to erect a barrier to the exercise of a constitutional right.

Such, he implied, was what had transpired in the pocket veto case.

In support of this view, the chief justice drew on a source who may be familiar to the reader, the long-term Texas Democratic congressman and now chair of the House Committee on the Judiciary, Hatton Sumners. He had been an amicus curiae in the 1928 pocket veto litigation, with his brief praised but also rejected by Justice Sanford. Now Chief Justice Hughes quoted in some detail from Sumners's brief, and he added that "the fact that Mr. Sumners' contention in the Pocket Veto Case was unavailing with respect to the effects of an adjournment of the Congress at the close of its regular session, in no way detracts from the pertinence and cogency of these observations as addressed to the situation which is now presented."

One reason why Hughes might have found the Sumners brief more persuasive then had been the case with his predecessors rests in the hypothetical the congressman had mentioned. Where the Senate was not available, "the sensible thing to do in such a case, would be for the messenger of the President, finding himself unable to make delivery to the Senate, to make the delivery to the Secretary of the Senate. There is nothing in the Constitution to prohibit that from being done." What had been a hypothetical in the 1929 argument turned into reality for the 1938 litigation. Moreover, Hughes continued, the chief if not the sole basis for the contention that the bill could not be "returned by the President during the Senate's recess is our decision in the Pocket Veto Case." But Hughes stated that "we do not regard that decision as applicable for two reasons: (1) The present question was not involved; and (2) the reasoning of the decision is inapposite [*sic*] to the circumstances of this case."

In 1929 the court had addressed itself to an instance where there had been an adjournment by both houses of Congress. Indeed, it was not in session from July 3 to December 2, 1926, a period of about five months. But the justices, insisted Hughes, "did not decide, and there was no occasion for ruling, that the [adjournment] clause applies where the

Congress has not adjourned and a temporary recess has been taken by one House," while the session of Congress continued. In other words, what the court confronted in 1938 differed from what it had resolved in 1929. To be sure, Sanford had ruled that "no return can be made to the House when it is not in session as a collective body and its members are dispersed." Here again Hughes modified the 1929 holding. That expression, he wrote, "should not be construed so narrowly as to demand that the President must select a precise moment when the House is within the walls of its chambers and that a return is absolutely impossible during a recess however temporary."

The chief justice reiterated the concern of the 1929 Taft Court that after adjournment a bill might be delivered to "some individual officer or agent not authorized to make any legislative record of its delivery, who should hold it in his hands for days, weeks or perhaps months." In fact, Congress had adjourned for a period of some five months. Perhaps, the chief justice conceded, given the facts in the pocket veto case, the Taft Court might have been correct to mention "the dangers which the Court envisaged." But 1929 was not 1938, and "however real these dangers may be when Congress has adjourned and the members of it have dispersed," they "appear to be illusory when there is a mere temporary recess" of three days or less. In the *Wright* case, the officers of the Senate continued to function without interruption, and with the bill properly safeguarded for a very limited time, the prospect that it "will not be subject to reasonably prompt action by the House is, we think, wholly chimerical."

Finally, Hughes turned again to the *Wright* case and held that "the question now raised has not been the subject of judicial decision." Yet it "must be resolved not by past uncertainties, assumptions or arguments, but by the application of the controlling principles of constitutional construction." What of the possibility of a future case where, unlike here, one house consents to a long period of adjournment by the other? Hughes dismissed this possible scenario out of hand. "We have no such case before us, and we are not called upon the conjecture as to the nature of the action which might be taken by the Congress in such a case, or what would be its effect." In this case, however, Congress had not adjourned, and the Senate wherein the bill had originated was in recess for three days. FDR received the bill on April 24. The ten-day period allotted to him expired on May 6. The Senate had adjourned for a three-day recess beginning on May 4, to reconvene on May 7. Roosevelt delivered the bill replete with his objections on May 5, still within the prescribed ten days. The Senate did not reconvene until May 7. The bill's ultimate fate was due to Congress's inaction.

Although counsel for Wright had argued vigorously to the contrary, Chief Justice Hughes found that Roosevelt had indeed acted within the law. In the absence of the Senate, he had delivered the bill with his objections to the appropriate Senate official, and in response the Senate had merely referred it to the Committee on Claims. Beyond this, neither House nor Senate appears to have taken up the bill again. "In this instance," concluded the chief justice, "the bill was properly returned by the President. It was open to reconsideration in Congress." Such reconsideration did not take place, and thus the bill "did not become a law."

* * *

While Hughes received unanimous accord from his colleagues on his point that the Senate bill had not become law, two justices questioned his reasoning in reaching this conclusion. Harlan Stone, joined by Louis Brandeis, emphasized that the vetoed bill had died not because it was submitted to the Senate within the ten-day period. Rather, it was because "the Senate by its adjournment had prevented the return" and thus triggered the provision that the bill could not survive where adjournment had blocked its return to the house of origin. Indeed, the reasoning of Hughes in reaching his conclusion "seem[s] to me to have no application to the [*Wright*] case . . . and leave in confusion and doubt the meaning and effect of the veto provisions . . . the certainty of whose application is of supreme importance." Stone acknowledged further that each house of Congress conceivably could "confer upon its secretary, Clerk or some other officer, authority to receive a bill returned to it by the President."

But this possibility was more than offset by its utter lack of probability. "It does not appear that any such authority has ever been conferred on the Secretary of the Senate, or that he has hitherto assumed to act in that capacity." Indeed, "there has been no action and no usage of either House recognizing the existence of such authority in any one." Whatever "constitutional power the [Congress] may possess to designate an officer to receive in their behalf bills returned by the President, they have not exercised it." Neither "the Constitution, nor any statute, rule or usage has indicated any person who could so act." In short, the pronouncement from the chief justice that the secretary of the Senate could receive a return from the president was without constitutional legitimacy.

Stone found it difficult—if not impossible—to reconcile the majority opinion in this case with the pocket veto decision of 1929. If Sanford had been mistaken in barring a three-day adjournment from coverage under the veto clauses, the "decision was wrong, and in the interests of a definite and precise constitutional procedure in a field where definiteness and precision are of paramount importance, it should now be frankly overruled." Moreover, Stone added, "if the experience of one and fifty years of constitutional interpretation has taught any lesson, it is the unwisdom, of making solemn declarations as to the meaning of that instrument which are unnecessary to decision. They can serve no useful purpose, and their only effect may be to embarrass the Court when decision becomes necessary." In particular, Stone objected to the reading of the Constitution that barred adjournment of one house for two or three days from constitutional legitimacy in terms of the veto power. Such an interpretation "finds its only support in a punctilio of grammar."

Further, added Stone, as Chief Justice Hughes had amply demonstrated by 1938, the court "has consistently held that a literal reading of a provision of the Constitution which defeats a purpose evident when the instrument is read as a whole, is not to be favored. The phrase 'due process' . . . has long since been expended [*sic*] beyond its literal meaning," just as the contract clause "is not literally confined to a law dictionary." No one should know this better than Hughes, Stone implied, citing the chief's famous holding that the prohibition against impairment of contracts has never been "taken to be inexorable." So too, "the injunction that no person shall be compelled in any criminal case to be a witness against himself is not literally applied." Constitutional provisions "are not to be interpreted like those of a municipal code or of a penal statute. . . . They are to be read as a vital part of an organic whole so that the high purpose which illumines every sentence and phrase of the instrument may be given effect in a harmonious frame-work of government."

Here, Stone echoed the well-known views of his colleague Justice Brandeis, who joined Stone's partial dissent. Had the court followed his argument, Hughes would not have insisted "that the phrase 'unless the

Congress by their adjournment prevent its return' cannot be taken to include the adjournment of [a] single House." Instead, the chief justice had emphasized that the word 'Congress' "followed as it is by the plural possessive pronoun 'their' can only refer to the two Houses . . . and hence cannot refer to adjournment of a single House." Stone strongly objected to such a view. "This subordination of the framers' main objective to a meticulously grammatical interpretation of their words is unwarranted." "I cannot hold," Stone concluded, "that for no discernable reason other than our present day notions of grammatical construction we are compelled to read the words as excluding from the operation of the [veto] clauses designed to protect the veto power, every case where the return of a bill is prevented by adjournment of a single House."

In summary, several points need to be made about these two decisions. In the first place, with the *Wright* case, all Chief Justice Hughes actually held was that FDR had not been prevented from vetoing the Senate bill. His action had *not* been a pocket veto because in fact he had returned the bill to the appropriate house along with his objections. Under these conditions, Hughes intimated that a pocket veto probably would have been unconstitutional, as the Congress had not prevented a return of the bill. Roosevelt's return had been timely, and the Senate had failed to reconsider the measure, thereby effectively killing it. Yet in one respect Hughes went beyond Sanford's 1929 findings.

He used broad language in holding further that an adjournment of a few days for the Senate—with its counterpart still in session—did not prevent the president from returning the bill to an agent or in this case the secretary of the Senate. Thus, he moved the court past Sanford's original insistence that the return had to be to a house in active session, with its elected leadership functioning. Hughes pointed to the fact that Sanford had been concerned with unfortunate effects from an adjournment that in fact had lasted more than five months, while the *Wright* case had involved a recess for only three days. The pocket veto case concerned action (actually it was inaction) taken by Coolidge in 1926 during an *intersession* of Congress, while in 1936 FDR returned the bill during a congressional *intrasession*, with the Senate adjourned for a maximum of three days.

A few words about the context in which *Wright* was decided may be appropriate as this chapter concludes. In early 1938 Roosevelt was in the midst of his second term, having been reelected in 1936 with the greatest margin of winning votes thus far recorded for a presidential candidate. However, throughout much of 1937, FDR and Congress had been embroiled in a bitter, partisan, and divisive battle over his famous (or infamous) "court-packing plan." By the end of the year it had been rejected, resulting in a major defeat for a president well known for his legislative legerdemain. Of course, the nine members of the high court were fully aware of the controversy as they handed down the *Wright* decision in January 1938.

This holding fully vindicated Roosevelt's action, even as it transformed the earlier 1929 pocket veto holding. It is, in the end, writes Jeff Shesol, "impossible to know what sways a judge. Even the judges themselves do not always know whether their decisions are driven, in the main, by doctrine or emotion, by the dictates of law or politics or conscience." Justices can be susceptible "to influence by legal briefs, oral arguments, pressure from their peers, and not least national events." Perhaps it may be a combination of them all.

PART III

Beyond the Pocket Veto Case

CHAPTER 7

Digging Deeper into the Pocket Veto Cases, 1970–1987

More often than not, law tends to ratify rather than innovate. The correctness of this generalization may be seen in legal developments concerning the pocket veto in the half century since the 1929 holding first affirmed this practice. Thus, the opinion by Justice Edward Sanford for a unanimous court might be considered more as ratification rather than innovation. The key holding simply affirmed as constitutional a practice that had been in use among chief executives since 1812. In a similar vein, the conclusion that a bill must be returned to the house of origin while in session merely ratified long-standing congressional practice. Again, the assertion that adjournment meant more than a final cessation of a particular Congress echoed long-established legislative preference.

Justice Sanford's opinion also reflected his awareness of time as a significant factor in the context of the pocket veto. In this case, Congress had adjourned for approximately five months. Apparently, the framers had not considered nor could the Taft Court envisage the possibility that a vetoed bill might be returned to some congressional official "who should hold it in his own hands for days, weeks or perhaps months . . . keeping the bill in the meantime in a suspended state of animation until the House resumes its sitting." Between 1929 and 1938 when *Wright v. United States* was decided, a major transformation took place in congressional scheduling. With the ratification of the Twentieth Amendment in January 1933, Congress now met on January 3 of each year, and the "lengthy adjournments between the first and second sessions" disappeared. Thus by the time *Wright* had been briefed and argued, congressional adjournments of five months no longer took place. The major concern of the Taft Court in its 1929 holding had ceased to exist.

When deciding the *Wright* case, the Hughes Court distinguished but did not overrule the earlier pocket veto decision. In a number of other cases, Chief Justice Hughes had done just that. Here, to a marked extent he reduced the reach and significance of Sanford's holding. In 1929 there had been an adjournment of five months. In 1936 the Senate had taken a recess of three days. Moreover, the House had not adjourned at all but was still in session. Since Congress had not adjourned, the pocket veto could not be implemented, and its consideration formed no part of Hughes's decision. He simply held that the president had been able to deliver the bill to the house of origin, in this case the Senate, within the requisite period of time.

Nor did the fact that the Senate had not yet returned from its three-day recess trouble the chief justice. Echoing and endorsing the earlier view of Hatton Sumners, who had argued for the House Committee on the Judiciary as an amici in the pocket veto case, Hughes emphasized that there was "no practical difficulty in returning the bill during a recess." In holding to the contrary, the Taft Court had managed "to ignore the plainest practical considerations and by implying a requirement of an artificial formality to erect a barrier to the exercise of a constitutional right." In this case, Hughes insisted, "there is no withholding of the bill from appropriate legislative record for weeks or perhaps months, no keeping of the bill in a state of suspended animation with no certain knowledge on the part of the public whether it was seasonably delivered, no causing of any undue delay in its reconsideration." Over time, the fears Sanford found so disturbing in 1929 had dissipated.

For Hughes, the "length of an adjournment was an important concern of the Court." Yet he refused to consider the possibility that if one house consents to a longer adjournment than three days, "a long period of adjournment may result." In fact, "we have no such case before us and we are not called upon to conjecture as to the nature of the action which might be taken by the Congress in such a case or what would be its effect." The chief justice also declined to consider the constitutionality of the pocket veto during an intrasession of Congress, as was the case in *Wright*, contrasted with an intersession of Congress, as was the case in 1929. Holding that in the *Wright* case President Roosevelt had complied with the law, he left the issue of the pocket veto exercised during an intrasession of Congress to be decided at a later day. That day arrived in December 1970, within the first term of President Richard Nixon.

* * *

The third episode of federal judicial involvement with Congress, the president, and the pocket veto began on December 14, 1970, when the legislature presented S. 3418 to Richard Nixon along with the requisite ten-day period for his examination. Nixon had until December 24 to return the bill. S. 3418 had passed both houses by overwhelming (and veto-proof) margins, 64–1 in the Senate and 346–2 in the House. It authorized Congress to appropriate some $225 million for grants to hospitals and medical schools to increase special departments and programs in the field for the family practice of medicine. Eight days after the bill had been presented to Nixon, on December 22, both houses adjourned for the Christmas holidays, the Senate until December 28 and the House until December 29. As they were each longer than three days, both houses had consented to the adjournments. Further, the secretary of the Senate by unanimous vote had been authorized to receive messages from the president.

Ten days after he had received the bill, barely within his permissible time frame and with both houses still in adjournment, Nixon not only failed to return the bill but also "issued a memorandum of disapproval and announced that he was withholding his approval from S. 3418." He took no further action, and the ten-day period quietly passed into oblivion. In due course Senator Edward Kennedy, who from the record appears to have represented himself, filed suit in the Federal District Court for the District of Columbia, seeking two actions from it: 1st, that the court issue a declaratory judgment that the Family Practice of Medicine Act "became a validly enacted law of the United States on December 25, 1970, without the signature of the President," and 2d, that it order the appropriate government officials "to publish S. 3418 as a validly enacted law of the United States." Kennedy, a Democrat from Massachusetts, had been elevated to the Senate in 1962, replacing his brother who had been elected president. He would be returned to his seat for an additional eight terms, a record that remains unequaled in Massachusetts.

The reader may recall that William Lewis had asked the Court of Claims to order payment of certain claims to the Indian tribes he represented, only to be blocked by a preliminary legal maneuver to dismiss his case, one that turned out to be decisive. Here also, Senator Kennedy faced a preliminary effort to bar consideration of his case. It included, among other assertions, a second legal maneuver dealing with the question of standing, that is, the legal right of a plaintiff to seek relief in a federal court of law. The Justice Department insisted that Senator Kennedy lacked standing to maintain his claim; that the president "is an indispensable party who cannot be sued"; and finally that the issue raised by Kennedy did not present a substantial case or controversy for two reasons: first, that it is a nonjusticiable "political question," and second, that Kennedy was seeking an "advisory opinion," both matters not acceptable in federal court.

A key element in resolving a question of standing is that it "focuses on the party seeking to get his complaint before a federal court and not on the issues he wishes to have adjudicated." In this case, "the question is whether the person [Senator Kennedy] whose standing is challenged is a proper person to request an adjudication of a particular issue and not whether the issue itself is justiciable." Plaintiff must demonstrate that the actions of President Nixon have caused him "injury in fact, economic or otherwise." He must also show that the right(s) he seeks to have protected by the court are "arguably within the zone of interests to be protected by the statute or constitutional guarantee in question." According to Judge Joseph Waddy, Kennedy succeeded in confronting both these challenges.

Judge Waddy turned first to the injury Kennedy claimed to have suffered by Nixon's use of the pocket veto. Such action "was an unconstitutional act that rendered Kennedy's vote in the Senate for the bill ineffective[,] and deprived him of his constitutional right to vote to override the Presidential Veto in an effort to have the bill passed without the President's signature." This "claim of nullification of his vote for the bill and deprivation of his right to vote to override the veto and thus inhibiting him in performance of his Senatorial duties, is a clear allegation of injury in fact." Given the huge majorities by which this bill had cleared Congress, Nixon could only have been well aware that the vote to override any traditional veto he might exercise would almost certainly be successful. Such awareness might have impelled him to attempt a pocket veto, thus avoiding a confrontation with the Senate. Waddy ruled that protection of this senator's right to vote "is . . . arguably within the zone of interests" to receive constitutional protection. Again, the rightness or wrongness of Kennedy's complaint at this point did not concern the judge, only that the senator had demonstrated sufficient standing to raise it, and the judge so ruled.

But the defendants had raised a second objection to Kennedy's complaint, that Nixon as president "is an indispensable party to this suit. Therefore the Court lacks jurisdiction" over him. Again, Waddy considered the point to be unpersuasive. Kennedy's complaint and the relief he sought "do not require any jurisdiction by the court over the President." Moreover, "the order requested by [Kennedy] requires no action by the President." Indeed, whatever Nixon did or did not do, his action "is complete upon the expiration of the ten-day Constitutional period. The time for deliberation has passed. He has decided. His judgment has been made, and the status of the legislation has been determined." All that remained is that the appropriate federal officers be ordered to carry out their "ministerial, non-discretionary duty" of publishing the acts that have since become federal laws.

This principle, added Waddy, "has been settled law" since the celebrated case of *Marbury v. Madison* in 1803. Mandamus is indeed "an appropriate remedy to require subordinate federal officers to carry out their ministerial duties." In this case, such a function did not involve the president in any way. Waddy cited the two previous Supreme Court decisions prominent in this case. He noted that "the President was not a party to either of them, and the Supreme Court exercised its jurisdiction and so decided on the merits without considering the absence of the President as a party." There remained one other preliminary claim by the government, that Kennedy's suit did not represent a substantial case or controversy.

Waddy demonstrated no difficulty in rejecting this assertion. He assumed, as did Kennedy, that cases or controversies "limit the business of federal courts to questions presented in an adversary context and in a form historically viewed as capable of resolution through the judicial process." To be sure, the restriction to "cases and controversies" has been accepted as consistently "imposing a rule against advisory opinions." But Kennedy had never sought an advisory opinion. On the contrary, he had "sponsored, supported, and voted for S. 3418." Nixon "in disapproving [the bill as well as] the injury to plaintiff by the refusal of the defendants to perform their ministerial nondiscretionary duties . . . provide[s] exactly the sort of clear concreteness, precise framing of questions, adversary argument, conflicting and demanding interests, and necessity for decision that have always been regarded as meeting the [constitutional] requirement for the exercise of Federal judicial power."

On rejecting every one of the several challenges the defendants had raised in order to prevent Kennedy's suit from being heard, finally Waddy was able to turn to the merits. Having allowed Kennedy to prevail on each of the preliminary contentions raised against his suit, one is not surprised that ultimately this jurist found in his favor. He relied heavily on *Wright v. United States*. The key question was where a bill had been passed by Congress and submitted to the president "and thereafter . . . by mutual consent the House . . . adjourned for a 6 day period and the Senate . . . for a 5 day period extending 2 days beyond the 10th day the President had within which to sign or return the bill, [did such action prevent] the President . . . from returning the bill within the 10 day period," given the Senate's specific instructions to receive messages from the chief executive? Waddy concluded "that the answer to that question is in the negative." He emphasized, as had Chief Justice Hughes, that the earlier court decision in 1929 "applied to an adjournment [of some five months] at the end of a session and not to a short [and temporary] recess during a session where, as here, the Senate had specifically authorized its Secretary to receive messages from the President during the recess."

Waddy noted of the court's reasoning in *Wright* that a short and temporary recess of a house on the final day for the return of a bill does not "prevent" the president "from returning the bill is clearly applicable to the facts and circumstances of [Kennedy's] case. Here we have a short temporary recess of the Senate . . . extending at most for two days beyond the 10th day the President had in which to act." Its "officers and organization continued to function without interruption," and "just as none of the dangers envisaged by the Court in the *Pocket Veto Case* were present in *Wright*, none are present here." The *Wright* case had made it clear that a short and temporary recess by House or Senate did not in itself prevent a return of a bill from the president. Here, Nixon had indicated to the Senate on December 24, "one day before the expiration of the time allowed for his consideration," that he opposed the bill. Had he returned the bill, it would have awaited the Senate, which reconvened on December 28 and did not adjourn *sine die* until January 2, 1971.

Hence the president had ample opportunity to return the bill, and had he done so, the Senate would have had reasonable time to reconsider his veto. Therefore, Nixon's action can in no way be considered a pocket veto. But Senator Kennedy asked that Judge Waddy go further and "hold that the Pocket veto is applicable only to *sine die* (final) adjournments and not to any adjournments within a session." Possibly considering in this sole instance that *Wright* was wrong, Waddy responded that "such a holding is not necessary for the determination of this case, and this Court declines to swim in waters that the Supreme Court pointedly avoided in *Wright.*" All that the district court decided was that Nixon had *not* been prevented from returning the bill by the temporary recess of the Senate. The president had chosen not to return the bill, and as the ten days expired, so did his opportunity to employ the pocket veto. S. 3418 thus became law. The Nixon administration promptly appealed to the US Court of Appeals for the DC circuit.

* * *

Delivering the unanimous opinion of the appellate panel, Judge Edward Tamm first had to confront anew the issue of standing. Even though Kennedy had not been authorized to prosecute his suit on behalf of either Congress or the Senate, the jurist held, as had Judge Waddy, that plaintiff "has standing to maintain this suit . . . as a United States Senator who voted in favor of S. 3418." A logical nexus existed "between the status asserted by a litigant and the claim sought to be adjudicated." On appeal, however, the United States claimed that Kennedy's vote in favor of the Senate bill "has no legal significance independent of the other votes in favor of the bill." Any injury to him, if indeed one occurred, "is derivative in nature." Only the Senate or Congress as a group had "sustained the direct injury necessary to confer standing," and Kennedy "is not" the Senate.

Tamm conceded that this observation "is undoubtedly correct but it does not help appellants' argument." The prerequisite to standing is that a party "be among the injured, not that he be the most grievously or most directly injured." There can be no doubt that Kennedy was among the injured in this case. Nixon's view of the expansive power in the pocket veto "threatens a diminution of congressional influence in the legislative process. It seems to this court axiomatic that, to the extent that Congress' role in the government is thus diminished, so too must be the individual roles of each of its members." In effect, Kennedy argued that Nixon's conduct "amounted to an illegal nullification not only of Congress' exercise of its power, but also [Kennedy's] exercise of his power." Indeed, Kennedy filed this suit so as to "vindicate the effectiveness of his vote. No more essential interest could be asserted by a legislator."

Having reaffirmed Kennedy's standing to bring his suit, Tamm turned to the merits. The panel was convinced that "an intrasession adjournment of Congress does not prevent the President from returning a bill . . . so long as appropriate arrangements are made for the receipt of presidential messages during the adjournment." Such had happened in this case, and thus the Court of Appeals affirmed Waddy's earlier finding that S. 3418 had become a law without Nixon's approval. Tamm recalled Chief Justice Hughes's insistence in the *Wright* case that the two purposes reflected in the veto provisions of the Constitution should be respected: (1) that the president shall have suitable opportunity to consider the bills presented to him, and (2) that the Congress shall have suitable opportunity to consider his objections. "We should not," Hughes had stated, "adopt a construction which would frustrate either of these purposes."

Tamm added that "where possible, then, the pocket veto clause should be construed in a manner which preserves both purposes. Since a pocket veto always has the effect of frustrating Congress' right to reconsider a vetoed bill, the preferred construction of the clause is that return of a bill was not 'prevented' by an adjournment." Such had been the key part of the *Wright* decision. It had held that a return of a bill during an intrasession can "be accomplished by delivery to an appropriate agent" of the originating house. What might have been possible in 1938 appeared as an actual result in 1974. "The mere fact," Tamm concluded, "that the Senate was not in session to physically receive the President's objections does not require the conclusion that the Congress had, by its adjournment prevented the return of S. 3418."

At this point in his opinion, Tamm turned to some relevant congressional history. He emphasized once again that the intersession at issue in 1929 had been one of five months. "By contrast," he noted only "four intrasession adjournments in the history of the Congress have exceeded six days in duration," and only two of them occurred in the twentieth century. "Plainly, intrasession adjournments of Congress have virtually never occasioned interruptions of the magnitude considered in the

Pocket Veto Case." Until the *Sampson* case, any uncertainty "arises from the absence of a definitive ruling as to whether an intrasession adjournment prevents the return of a vetoed bill. Hopefully, our present opinion eliminates that ambiguity."

To be sure, a number of intrasession pocket vetoes have occurred, mostly since 1933. But, and here Tamm drew on an argument presented by William Lewis in the original pocket veto case, "consistent practice cannot create or destroy an executive power," especially when one considers that the intrasession pocket veto is "a relatively new phenomenon." Indeed, the instant case "arises from the shortest intrasession ever relied upon by any President as having prevented the return of a disapproved bill." Tamm turned to the ultimate question of "whether any intrasession adjournment, as that practice is currently understood, can prevent the return of a bill . . . where appropriate arrangements have been made for receipt of presidential messages during the adjournment—a question which must be answered in the negative." Thus, because Nixon had failed to return the bill as he could have, S. 3418 became law ten days after it had been submitted to him.

But the August 1974 unanimous decision by the Court of Appeals that sustained the claims of Senator Kennedy did not end the pocket veto controversy. Nixon employed the same tactic again on a transportation bill. His pocket veto had come between the first and second sessions of the Ninety-Third Congress, a period of some twenty-nine days. Thus it was an intercession veto. Yet by midsummer, Nixon had more pressing concerns. August saw the Watergate crisis in full flower, with Nixon resigning from office on August 8. Senator Kennedy described this pocket veto as a direct "flouting" of Tamm's opinion. Meanwhile, in October, Nixon's successor, Gerald Ford, pocket vetoed an "Aid to the Handicapped" bill, this one during the thirty-one-day intrasession for the fall congressional elections. Kennedy filed suit once again, challenging both of these vetoes.

As it had previously sought, albeit without success, the United States moved to dismiss Kennedy's suit on the by-now-familiar grounds that he lacked standing. Early in January 1976 the case came before district court judge John Sirica, himself of recent Watergate distinction. Sirica wasted no time on the issue of standing. "This argument of the defendants is entirely without merit, [as] the United States Court of Appeals for the District of Columbia Circuit has already squarely addressed this issue." Moreover, accepting by implication Kennedy's claim that the two bills in question had become law without presidential approval, he further ruled that the defendants had not published the two "laws" as was required, and he refused to dismiss Kennedy's suit. It lay pending for several months.

Although he did not explain why, possibly in the wake of the Watergate episode, in April President Ford capitulated to the position taken by Kennedy. On April 13, the Justice Department announced that "it will no longer oppose a suit [brought by Senator Kennedy] questioning the scope of presidential authority to use the pocket veto." The announcement added that the president "will use the return veto rather than the pocket veto during [both] intrasession and intersession recesses and adjournments of the Congress," provided that whichever house to which the president's objections must be returned "has specifically authorized an officer or other agent to receive return vetoes during such periods." Two weeks later, Kennedy spoke to his colleagues, and perhaps he can be pardoned if he appeared somewhat enthusiastic in tone.

Ford's recent action, according to Kennedy, "is a generous and complete vindication of the rights of Congress and its role in the enactment of Federal legislation, and I welcome the President's decision." Kennedy did not state that in the second of the two bills at issue in the case before Sirica, the adjournment had been an intersession, not intrasession. Nor, for that matter, did the lawyers for the administration. Faced with such a capitulation, Kennedy had promptly moved for summary judgment, a motion in which Ford's lawyers concurred. On April 21 Judge Sirica ordered that "the plaintiff's motion for summary judgment be, and the same hereby is, granted." Thus it would have appeared that the president is barred from applying a pocket veto during a brief intrasession, where his messages can be readily received. The word "brief" should be noted, for in itself the pocket veto remains a legitimate part of constitutional law. Meanwhile, in 1982 Theodore Olsen, serving as an assistant attorney general in the Office of General Counsel, put the matter very well. "We would recommend," he wrote, "that the President not pocket veto legislation during intrasession adjournments unless he is willing to risk an almost certain court challenge in which he may not be successful. ... We would advise that the President not pocket veto bills unless the intrasession adjournment involved extends for a significant period of time—ten days at least."

Later reflecting on his victory, in 1977 Senator Kennedy assumed that since his two favorable court decisions, "the pocket veto power is unavailable to the President during any intrasession adjournments and during brief intersession adjournments," as well. As for the high court's unanimous finding in the pocket veto case almost half a century before Kennedy wrote, that case "has been confined to its facts," and if the intrasession pocket veto has become unconstitutional, "the intersession pocket veto has become an obsolete relic." He stated, however, that "neither *Sampson* nor *Jones* carries the precedential authority of a Supreme Court Decision." A future administration could choose to relitigate the issue in the federal courts. Perhaps Kennedy wrote with greater prescience than he realized. Barely six years later, one did.

*   *   *

It can be said that a situation confronting President Ronald Reagan and Congress in the fall of 1983 has an interesting ring of familiarity to it. On September 30 the House passed a bill (H.R. 4042) extending certain certification requirements concerning restrictions on military assistance and sales to El Salvador. On November 17 the Senate concurred without any amendments. One day later, congressional officials signed off on the bill, which was presented to the president on November 18. Later that same day, the Ninety-Eighth Congress adjourned its first session *sine die* and agreed to reconvene for its second session on January 23, 1984, some nine weeks later. Both houses had provided for the reception of presidential messages by the appropriate congressional officials. On November 30, the last day open to the president for returning the bill, Reagan neither signed the measure nor returned it to the House with his objections. Instead, he issued a statement that he was withholding his approval of the bill. Accordingly, government officials refused to deliver the bill as required and publish it as a federal law. A few weeks later, members of Congress drawn from both houses filed suit.

Plaintiffs sought a declaratory judgment that H.R. 4042 had indeed become a "validly enacted law of the United States" and a mandamus that it "be published as a public law." Early in his opinion, however, Judge Thomas Jackson indicated that he would simply follow the pocket veto case of 1929. It had focused on the question of whether a bill passed by both houses and presented to the president fewer than ten days prior to adjournment "but is neither signed by the President nor returned by him . . . becomes a law in like manner as if he had signed it." In a unanimous decision, the Supreme Court had "answered the question in the negative, and since it is identical to the question presented by the instant case, so must this court." Further, Jackson was not persuaded that either *Wright* or *Sampson* "have so attenuated *Pocket Veto* as to deprive it of controlling force here."

In the first place, the *Wright* case did not involve the pocket veto, as Congress had not formally adjourned. Moreover, in *Sampson*, Congress had taken a brief recess for a five-day intrasession, something far different from the five months involved in the 1929 holding. Indeed, its ruling was limited "to an intrasession adjournment (which had been, in fact, of only five days duration)," while the instant case involved an adjournment of some eight weeks or so. Thus Jackson held that "neither *Wright* nor *Kennedy v. Sampson* give [him] license to depart from the only case directly in point, *Pocket Veto*. Unless and until the Supreme Court reconsiders the rule of that case, this Court must, as must all lower federal courts, follow it." Denied their motion for summary judgment and injunctive relief, plaintiffs promptly appealed to the Circuit Court of Appeals for the DC Circuit, where *Sampson* had been finally decided in 1974.

Three judges heard arguments on June 4, 1984, and decided the case in August, with formal opinions filed in April 1985. The panel split two to one, with the majority finding for the plaintiffs and reversing Judge Jackson. Judge Robert Bork, for whom the future held Senate rejection of his appointment to the Supreme Court in 1987, dissented but did not reach the merits of the case, focusing instead on the sole issue of plaintiffs' standing to file suit. While his dissent was detailed and lengthy, it lacked an essential ingredient. Bork failed to convince his brethren.

Speaking for himself and Chief Judge Spottswood Robinson, Senior Circuit Judge Carl McGowan identified the plaintiffs in this case. They consisted of "thirty-three individual members of the House . . . joined by the United States Senate," as well as the House Speaker and "the bipartisan leadership of the House." If one individual senator had possessed standing, as had been true of Kennedy in the earlier litigation, than surely a greater number of legislators could only have the same right, all the more as "in the present action, the thirty-three Representatives allege an injury identical to that of the individual lawmaker in *Kennedy v. Sampson.*" Since the panel had reversed Judge Jackson, this case remained good law. Thus "all the appellants are properly before this court." But before turning to the merits, Judge McGowan took advantage of the majority opinion coming first and offered a rebuttal to Bork's dissent even before that jurist could deliver it. "We wish to make clear the error in the dissent's understanding of Article III and the doctrine of separation of powers."

McGowan opened his comments on standing by citing Justice Lewis Powell, who in 1974 had warned that "repeated and essentially head-on confrontations between the life-tenured branch and the representative branches of government will not, in the long run, be beneficial to either." On the other hand, the judicial branch should "neither shrink from a confrontation with the other two coequal branches ... nor ... hospitably accept for adjudication claims of constitutional violation ... where the claimant has not suffered cognizable injury." Thus he rejected out of hand Robert Bork's "sweeping view that Article III bars any government plaintiff from litigating a claim of infringement of lawful function." To the contrary, insisted McGowan, "there could be no clearer instance of a constitutional impasse between the Executive and the Legislative branches than is presented by this case."

Here, Congress passed an act that the president neither signed nor returned but "has declared it not to be a law." Congress "has challenged the validity of that declaration." In so doing, the legislature is not seeking an advisory opinion from the court on some hypothetical question of constitutional law. Rather, it has focused on a "particular purported veto," which allegedly has done "a specific and concrete harm to its legislative powers," that is, "a deprivation of a constitutionally mandated process of enacting law that has actually occurred." That such injury "is judicially cognizable" has been clear since the Supreme Court so held in 1939. Indeed, "by defining the respective roles of the two branches in the enactment process, this court will help to preserve, not defeat, the separation of powers."

Turning to the merits of the *Barnes* complaint, McGowan found it necessary to reiterate the facts, arguments, and holdings in the previously decided pocket veto cases all over again. He especially emphasized the *Wright* and *Sampson* decisions. The 1938 case had two key points. Most important, its rule of construction "requires a court to find that the President was truly deprived of the opportunity" to use his veto power before it can hold that a return was "prevented." Second, without any doubt, the case "establishes that mere absence of the originating house does not prevent a return," if an appropriate congressional figure has been authorized "to accept delivery of a veto message." The 1974 *Sampson* decision simply extended *Wright* to hold that "return is not prevented by an intrasession adjournment of any length . . . so long as the originating house arranged for receipt of veto messages."

Finally, McGowan held that contemporary intercession adjournments no longer differ "in any practical respect from the intrasession adjournments at issue in" *Wright* and *Sampson*. Fully aware, as was his dissenting colleague Judge Bork, that McGowan's panel was about to reaffirm *Kennedy v. Sampson*, McGowan added that "of course . . . this panel is not free to reconsider a decision by another panel of this Court. Until it is overruled by the full court sitting *en banc*, *Kennedy v. Sampson* will remain the law of this Circuit." Thus the panel reversed Judge Jackson and ordered him to enter summary judgment for *Barnes* et al.

In a dissent that ran for more than thirty pages, Judge Bork failed to reach McCowan's holding on the merits. He was only concerned with that relatively brief part of the majority's decision that dealt with standing. From his perspective, of course if McGowan offered a wrong conclusion on that issue, as indeed he had according to Bork, there was no need to go any further. Bork reminded his reader that litigation between Congress and the president was unknown until his court "accepted the invitation to umpire such disputes," as it had with *Sampson*. Calling the circuit court's jurisprudence in these cases "a complete novelty," he insisted that "the direct intermediation of the courts in disputes between the President and Congress, ought to give us pause." More than that: "When reflection discloses that what we are asked to endorse is a major shift in basic constitutional arrangements, we ought to do more than pause. We ought to renounce outright the whole notion of congressional standing."

Particularly in this case, "the error in analysis produces an error in result." Indeed, "with a constitutional insouciance impressive to behold," various panels of the circuit court (but without the approval of the full court) have announced that they have jurisdiction to entertain lawsuits about governmental powers brought by congressmen against Congress or by congressmen against the president. That jurisdiction, however, "floats in midair. Any foundations it may once have thought to possess have long since been swept away by the Supreme Court." The net result is that "every time a court expands the definition of standing ... the area of judicial dominance grows and the area of democratic rule contracts. That is what is happening in this case." McGowan's opinion, according to his colleague, "represents a drastic rearrangement of constitutional structures, one that results in an enormous and uncontrollable expansion of judicial power." There is, Bork concluded, "not one shred of support for what the majority has done, not in the Constitution, in case law, in logic, or in any proper conception of the relationship to democracy."

Faced with a reversal of Judge Jackson's decision, lawyers for the federal officials charged with responsibility for the filing and ultimate publication of enacted bills first sought a rehearing en banc from the full DC circuit court. With Judges Bork, Scalia, and Starr dissenting, the court denied the petition on August 7, 1985. A few months later, counsel petitioned the high court for a writ of certiorari, hoping perhaps that the justices would wish to explore the major doctrinal disagreements between Judge McGowan's opinion and Judge Bork's emphatic dissent. On March 3, 1986, the high court granted the writ, and for the third time, the Supreme Court prepared to take up the matter of the pocket veto once again. It heard arguments on November 4, 1986.

Counsel for petitioners raised three key points, all of which had previously appeared in earlier litigation. First, he insisted that H.R. 4042 was now moot, even if somehow it had become a law as Judge McGowan had so held. The certification precondition imposed on military aid to El Salvador, however, had expired on September 30, 1984, more than two years before the court's action, and a matter of months before the Court of Appeals issued its opinions. Whether the bill ever became a law or not was irrelevant. "It plainly is not a law now, and no form of judicial relief can change that fact." Thus this case has now "lost its character as a present, live controversy ... of the kind that must exist if [the court] is to avoid advisory opinions on abstract propositions of law."

Moreover, ample case law indicated that a "challenge to a statute becomes moot when the statute is no longer in force." Thus, the high court should follow "its established practice of vacating the judgment below and remanding with a direction to dismiss." Further, respondents' emphasis on the compulsion to publish the law as enacted is misplaced. In fact, "the Constitution nowhere requires that a bill be published in the Statutes at Large in order for it to become as law." The statutes concerning publication "do not implement the constitutional design for the legislative process," and it is that process which is at issue in this case.

In the event that the justices did not find the claim of mootness to be persuasive, counsel turned to his second point, one that already had been litigated at some length in the circuit court. "Respondents do not have standing to obtain a judicial declaration that H.R. 4042 became a law." To be sure, the circuit court had found to the contrary, but its decision relied "on a doctrine of congressional standing unique to the District of Columbia Circuit." In fact, the doctrine of standing is built "on a single idea, the idea of separation of powers." This idea is wrongly challenged by a case such as this one, "in which a court is asked to referee an intragovernmental dispute between the political Branches . . . in the absence of any claim by a private party that he has been injured." The supposed injury suffered by Congress is in fact "merely a restatement of respondents' disagreement" with how the president interpreted the pocket veto provision.

In truth, according to counsel, "just as Congress cannot overrule Executive action directly by means of a legislative veto, Congress cannot accomplish the same result indirectly by invoking the assistance of the federal courts to prosecute its disagreement with the Executive." Further, respondents claim that they seek to enforce the responsibilities of those government officials to "preserve, publish, and make available copies of bills that have become laws." In reality, they seek to litigate "whether H.R. 4042 ever became a law," a very different question, and one that Congress and/or its houses and members would not have standing to raise. Finally, if the justices reject these two arguments, consideration of the merits should lead to a reversal of the circuit court, based on the reasoning of the unanimous holding in the 1929 pocket veto case.

Counsel for respondents, the House "Bipartisan Leadership Group," claimed that this case raised only two questions, both of which should be answered in the affirmative: (1) Whether the Court of Appeals was correct in recognizing that the "House and Senate parties" had standing "to redress the nullification of the lawmaking process" via the pocket veto, and (2) whether such veto was invalid because the House "had made adequate provision for return of the bill." This dispute between Congress and the president represented an example "where each branch has taken action asserting its constitutional authority—when, in short, the political branches reach a constitutional impasse." Finally, petitioners' contention that the case is moot "is without merit," and formal publication was warranted as H.R. 4042 had become law without the president's approval.

Here, "Executive Branch interference in the lawmaking of the Legislative Branch" has resulted in "an unavoidable conflict over the law. This is no internal problem of either Branch. It cannot be resolved by either official directives or collegial debate." Because no return came from the president, "Congress had nothing upon which to operate. With no further interchange, the two branches were frozen in their respective positions," resulting in "an immutable political logjam." Here is an instance where the high court must fulfill its duty "to say what the law is." It does not represent a political question, but rather it "presents a legal issue which this Court alone can resolve definitively." Further, "so long as the Congress allows the President his full ten days and does not prevent return or cut down his time, the Framers consigned the pace of the Congress's own resolution of a veto issue to the Congress, rather than to the President."

Finally, respondents insisted that the claim of mootness "is without merit." In fact, the petitioners "routinely publish all law enacted by the Congress, whatever their duration, including many that have expired." Petitioners "offer no cogent reason why this law, unlike all others, should go unpublished, only variations on their . . . argument against standing." Thus respondents urged the Supreme Court to affirm the circuit court's earlier decision that H.R. 4042 had become law.

The Supreme Court handed down its decision in *Burke v. Barnes* on January 14, 1987. Chief Justice Rehnquist noted that the bill in question had conditioned the continuance of military aid to El Salvador on the president's semiannual certification "of that nation's progress in protecting human rights." He further described the course of litigation that had ensued since the president neither signed nor returned the bill to its house of origin. Again, he summarized the three points emphasized by petitioners: (1) Respondents lacked standing, (2) the Court of Appeals had erred in its findings, and (3) the case is moot. Here, Rehnquist tacked on two sentences that could only have disappointed the attorneys for the members of Congress: the court held "that the case is moot. We therefore do not reach either of the other contentions of petitioners." Such a holding was bad enough for the respondents, but worse was yet to come.

There must be, according to the chief justice, "a live case or controversy at the time that a federal court decides the case." It is not sufficient that that there might have been such a case "when the case was decided by the court whose judgment we are reviewing." Any issues as to whether or not H.R. 4042 became a law "were mooted when that bill expired by its own terms." Whether or not there had been a pocket veto became irrelevant. The bill "became a dead letter on September 30, 1984, regardless of whether it had previously been enacted into law or not." Finally, Rehnquist observed that counsel for the respondents claimed that the failure of the petitioners to publish the law had caused the "nullification of their lawmaking processes." We "fail to see," the chief justice responded, "how any interest in the lawmaking process that might be served by the publication of duly enacted statutes can survive the life of the statutes themselves." For his six-member majority, Rehnquist ordered the case back to the Court of Appeals with "instructions to remand it to the District Court with instructions to dismiss the complaint."

But Rehnquist did not speak for a unanimous court. Justices Stevens and White considered the case far from moot. Stevens stated that if "the Legislature's interest in protecting its work from nullification by the Executive would have been sufficient to support standing prior to September 30, 1984, that interest is also sufficient to support standing today." Moreover, given the implications for continued aid to El Salvador, "as long as the question whether H.R. 4042 ever became a law continues to have practical significance, Congress retains its interest in ensuring that its enactments are given their proper legal effect." Finally, if the federal courthouse was a proper forum for resolution of the issues tendered prior to September 30, 1984—as indeed appears to have been the case— "it remains so today. Whatever else may be said about this case, it is not moot."

The case of *Burke v. Barnes* had offered the court an opportunity to resolve some of the difficult uncertainties that lingered in interpreting the pocket veto since the *Wright* case in 1938. But for reasons it chose not to explain, the justices punted, as it were, putting off until a later date dealing with the collective legacies of the pocket veto, *Wright*, and *Sampson* holdings. Instead, they reflected their agreement with Justice Louis Brandeis, who had emphasized that "the most important thing we do is not doing." Such a policy may contribute much to high court practice and preference. Yet it appears to have been of no value whatsoever to the six Indigenous tribes, with whom this story had started half a century before, in 1927.

Conclusion

This story of the pocket veto case, as is typical of much history concerning Native Americans, does not have a happy conclusion, at least for the six tribes who filed it. The pocket veto remains a part of the federal Constitution that received ratification in 1788. When William S. Lewis brought suit in the Court of Claims on their behalf in 1927, he probably had no inkling that his efforts to demand and receive federal compensation for loss of their lands would somehow become entangled in a critical dispute over the legitimacy of the pocket veto. This development has been detailed in these chapters. In the end, one of the interesting characteristics of my study is the total absence of the tribes as well as consideration of their claims from any of the judicial decisions analyzed therein. In terms of their legal significance, it is almost as if the six tribes did not exist. As he submitted his massive and detailed petition to the Court of Claims in March 1927, Lewis may well have looked forward to his day in court on behalf of the six Tribes. Yet counsel for the United States did not even respond to any of the points Lewis had raised. Indeed, the tribes' attorney appears never to have been able to argue them. Other legal issues formed the case he ultimately had to litigate, and the reasons for this unexpected result have been discussed in my study.

One might be sorely tempted to conclude, after reading what Lewis had drafted with such care on behalf of the tribes, that the ultimate outcome of his case should be seen as yet another all-too-typical example—out of so many available from which to choose—of the neglect, maltreatment, and cruelty inflicted on the tribes by the American legal order, and well documented by Walter Echo-Hawk. (See the bibliographic essay.) And indeed, this author gave brief consideration to such a conclusion. In retrospect, however, such an ending, while it might appeal to the emotions, would be incorrect as a matter of legal history as well as traditional trial law. The outcome of the pocket veto case and its aftermath was based on a legitimate and frequently employed legal tactic, the demurrer. This action in turn was built on the fact that Calvin Coolidge had exercised the pocket veto in his resolution of the bill he had received from Congress. In this he had followed a long line of American presidents beginning with James Madison.

The pocket veto case well demonstrates the transformative power of the legal process. After it first reached the federal court in 1927, the grievances of the six tribes became subsumed into major questions concerning the extent of constitutional authority shared by both Congress and the chief executive. These appeared to be much more important. When, if ever, was a pocket veto constitutional? What type of adjournment was required for it to be exercised? Did the pocket veto in fact represent a serious misinterpretation of executive authority? Did it in fact intrude on the legitimacy of congressional power? Finally, did the unquestioned continuation of its exercise for more than a century in any way contribute to its legitimacy? What unites all these issues is the total absence of the Indian tribes from their resolution. Between 1928 and 1938, both the Court of Claims and the Supreme Court considered and to some extent provided answers to these questions excluding, again, any discussion of the tribes.

Thus legal controversy over the pocket veto continued on, albeit without the original plaintiffs. Although the 1929 decision had been unanimous, in 1938 the high court took up the issue once again. This time, its decision came from a divided tribunal. While unanimous in their finding that President Roosevelt's actions had been constitutional, the justices could not agree on why. Chief Justice Hughes "distinguished" *Wright v. United States* from its predecessor. The pocket veto case had concluded that the term "adjournment" applied only when both houses of Congress had adjourned *sine die* at the conclusion of the congressional session, and further that when the president returned a bill to its house of origin, that body had to be in session. In 1938 Hughes held that it was constitutional for the president to return a bill to an authorized representative of either the House or the Senate when that body had either adjourned or was in recess. Because the Congress—as opposed to one house—had not formally adjourned, the pocket veto played no part in Hughes's decision. Both the *Wright* case and the earlier pocket veto decision as modified by Hughes have never been overruled.

Further, the pocket veto case retains its relevance for ongoing legal issues concerning separation of powers—a never-ending source of constitutional friction. In 1929 Justice Sanford had emphasized both the passage of time and legislative acquiescence as dual factors in legitimatizing pocket veto actions by the president. Some sixty years later, the high court upheld congressional enactment of the US Sentencing Commission. (See *Mistretta v. United States*, 488 U.S. 361 [1989].) Justice Harry Blackmun observed—as Justice Sanford had implied—that "traditional ways of conducting government . . . give meaning to the Constitution." Twenty-five years had elapsed when in 2014 a former member of the Sentencing Commission, now on the court himself, cited Sanford's pocket veto decision once again.

"Long settled and established practice," Justice Stephen Breyer recalled in quoting the pocket veto case, "is a consideration of great weight in a proper interpretation of constitutional provisions" especially when concerned with "the relationship between Congress and the President." (See *NLRB v. Canning*, 573 U.S. 513 [2014].) Breyer found further support in Sanford's statement that "a practice of at least twenty years duration on the part of the executive department, acquiesced in by the legislative department, . . . is entitled to great regard in determining the true construction of a constitutional provision, the phraseology of which is in any respect of doubtful meaning." The issue in *Canning* involved presidential appointments to fill vacancies "that initially occur before, but continue to exist during, a recess of the Senate." For many years, presidents have "interpreted the Recess Appointments Clause to apply to such vacancies, without objection from the Senate for nearly three quarters of a century, perhaps longer."

Repeatedly citing the pocket veto case, Breyer reiterated Sanford's earlier point that "there is a great deal of history to consider here." As Sanford had implied in 1929 when his court interpreted the pocket veto for the first time, so Breyer emphasized in 2014 that in interpreting the recess appointments clause for the first time, "we must hesitate to upset the compromises and working arrangements that the elected branches of Government themselves have reached," and "we are reluctant to upset this traditional practice where doing so would seriously shrink the authority that Presidents have believed existed and have exercised for so long." Thus the pocket veto case retains contemporary constitutional relevance, and separation of powers concerns remain important issues.

The Supreme Court appears not to have directly decided any further cases concerning the pocket veto other than the 1987 *Barnes* litigation, which had turned on the issue of mootness rather than offering any expanded constitutional analysis. However, in the cases of *Kennedy v. Sampson* and *Kennedy v. Jones*, the Court of Appeals for the District of Columbia had clarified the matter of a veto during a brief intrasession recess of Congress, as compared to an intersession adjournment. Because inherent tension between the president and Congress is built into our constitutional structure, there is always the potential for further litigation, and invariably the pocket veto case will be cited.

1791	First Amendment among those ratified as the Bill of Rights. It included a provision that forbade Congress from making any law abridging the right "to petition the Government for a redress of grievances." This provision could also be seen as a basis for the later creation of a new federal court.
1855	Establishment of a new federal Court of Claims, which provided for three new judges to be appointed by the president and granted life tenure. Any decisions the new court reached in its cases, however, depended on approval by the Congress before they could be implemented.
1863	After lengthy debate, a divided Congress voted to expand this court to include five judges, as well as ultimate authority to make its judgments final.
1872	President Ulysses S. Grant set aside land for an Indian reservation within what is now Washington State, the specific area being known as the Columbia Plateau. The Colville Reservation exists to this day, and it served as home to the six tribes who more than a half century later brought the lawsuit with which this book is concerned.
1881	Congress enacted the first special jurisdictional act relating to an Indigenous tribe (in this instance the Choctaw Nation) and authorized the Court of Claims to "take jurisdiction of and try all questions of differences arising out of treaty stipulations . . . and to render judgment thereon."
1924	The Indian Citizenship Act is passed and signed into law.
1925	Congress enacted a special bill authorizing several tribes within the state of Washington to bring suit against the United States. The bill failed, however, to identify the specific area of land or territory for which the tribes sought compensation, and it received a pocket veto from President Calvin Coolidge.
1926	Attorney William Lewis testified before both the House and Senate Subcommittees on Indian Affairs and detailed the past history of the tribes on whose behalf he sought enactment of another special bill authorizing a lawsuit in the Court of Claims.
1926	By voice vote Congress passed a special bill authorizing six tribes on the Colville Reservation to bring suit in the Court of Claims against the United States, and adjourned shortly thereafter.

1926	Assuming that a pocket veto was imminent if not a reality, William Lewis wrote to President Coolidge urging him to approve another version of this bill, should it reach his desk.
1926	Congress reconvened for its second session, and the House failed to pass another measure identical to the one pocket vetoed by President Coolidge.
1927	The Senate approved its own version of the House bill.
1927	The House debated whether or not a bill pocket vetoed by President Coolidge nevertheless in fact had become a law.
1927	On behalf of six tribes, William Lewis filed a petition of more than fifty pages in the Court of Claims, seeking more than $13 million allegedly owed to his clients by the United States.
1927	United States filed a demurrer to Lewis's petition.
1928	William S. Lewis filed a new brief of more than 130 pages "in resistance to Defendant's Demurrer."
1928	The Court of Claims heard arguments on Lewis's petition, and within three months the court unanimously sustained the demurrer.
1928	Lewis filed motion "for a rehearing and new trial" and submitted a "Supplemental Brief on Motion for a New Trial."
1928	The Court of Claims heard arguments on a new trial and one week later rejected Lewis's motion, apparently without written comment.
1928	Lewis filed a petition for a grant of certiorari before the US Supreme Court.
1928	President Coolidge transmitted a memorandum to Congress, "prepared in the office of the Attorney General regarding bills presented to the President less than ten days before the adjournment of Congress and not signed by him."
1929	The high court granted the writ of certiorari.
1929	Both Lewis and the United States submitted briefs to the Supreme Court in the case of *Okanogan Tribe et al. v. United States.*
1929	Congressman Hatton Sumners, Democrat from Texas, filed a brief as amicus curiae in this case.
1929	William Lewis, William Mitchell, and Hatton Sumners summarized their arguments before the US Supreme Court. See 279 U.S. 655 (1929).
1929	The high court unanimously sustained the original demurrer.
1936	Congress passed a special act enabling David Wright to file suit in the Court of Claims against the United States.

{ *Chronology* }

1936	President Roosevelt returned the bill unsigned with a veto message to the Senate, which was not in session to receive it. The Senate reconvened two days later.
1936	David Wright filed suit against the United States in the Court of Claims.
1936	The United States demurred to the suit, and the Court of Claims rejected Wright's petition, apparently without written opinion.
1937	Wright filed a petition for certiorari in the US Supreme Court, a step opposed by the Justice Department but granted by the high court.
1938	In *Wright v. United States*, 302 U.S. 583, the court unanimously held that the 1936 statute had not become a law and in so doing modified the 1929 *Okanogan* decision.
1973	*Kennedy v. Sampson*, 364 F. Supp. 1075 (1973), held that when appropriate arrangements had been made, an adjournment of the House and Senate for five or six days did not prevent the president from returning a bill.
1974	This decision was affirmed in *Kennedy v. Sampson*, 511 F.2d 430 (1974).
1776	President Ford announced he would "use the return veto rather than the pocket veto during [both] intrasession and intersession adjournments."
1984	*Barnes v. Carmen*, 582 F. Supp. 163 (1984), affirmed a pocket veto by President Reagan, but is reversed in *Barnes v. Kline*, 759 F.2d, 21 (1985).
1986	The Supreme Court granted certiorari in this case.
1987	The high court dismissed the case as moot on the grounds that the congressional statute involved had expired.

BIBLIOGRAPHIC ESSAY

Note from the series editors: The following bibliographic essay contains many primary and secondary sources the author consulted for this volume. We have asked all authors in this series to omit formal citations in order to make their volumes more readable, less expensive, and more appealing for students and general readers.

Before identifying the sources used in writing this study, a few preliminary observations may be appropriate. A complete bibliography of these materials is available in the manuscript copy of my volume, to be deposited in the Rutgers University Library Special Collections Department. This essay provides citations for works that shed light on the history of this case, that is, not only on how plaintiffs in the pocket veto case proposed to argue it but also on how the litigation ultimately came to be concluded. Most of them remain widely available either online or in university law libraries.

———

Part I: Primary Sources

Because, like other volumes in this series, this book involves a specific case—in this instance, cases—decided by the US Supreme Court, perhaps the place to begin in identifying source materials is with *The United States Supreme Court Records and Briefs*, an ongoing collection maintained in the Library of Congress, Legal Division. It is also available on microfilm. See Scholarly Resources, *Microfilm Edition of the Records and Briefs of the United States Supreme Court*. A more selective edition of records and briefs, but also much more readily available, is found in Phillip B. Kurland and Gerhard Casper, eds., *Landmark Briefs and Arguments of the Supreme Court of the United States* (University Publications of America, 1975). See volume 26, where the briefs and arguments of the pocket veto case may be examined. See 279 U.S. 655 (1929), and *Wright v. United States*, 302 U.S. 583 (1938). Other records and briefs of the remaining Supreme Court cases dealing with the pocket veto may be located in three databases: Gale: Primary Sources, *The Making of Modern Law—U.S. Supreme Court Records and Briefs, 1832–1978*; *Hein Online*; and Westlaw, *Campus Research*.

The six Indigenous tribes who collectively filed suit against the United States relied on a specific statute enacted by Congress in 1926, as well as an earlier piece of federal legislation that had created the Court of Claims in 1855, with additional revisions in 1862. An excellent background to these events is William Wiecek, "The Origins of the United States Court of Claims," 20 *Administrative Law Review* (1968). See also Newell Ellison, "The United States Court of Claims: Keeper of the Nation's Conscience for One Hundred Years," 24 *George Washington Law Review* (1956), and Winston Bowman, "A Brief History of the Court of Claims," *Federal Lawyer* (2016). Relevant congressional discussion and debate may be found in the *Congressional Globe* for the 37th Congress (1862). See also 37th Congress, 2d Sess., House Report #34, and *Appendix*, April 15, 1862. For the background to the 1926 statute, see 68th Cong., 2d sess., *House Report #1423*, also 69th Cong., 1st sess., *Hearings on H.R. 9270*, and *House Report #896*, "Indian Tribes to Present Claims . . ."

The would-be researcher into the origins of the special claims bill passed by Congress in 1926 should be aware that there is a great deal of valuable material in the relevant pages of the *Congressional Record*. Indeed, by 1926 the index to the *Record* had long been a significant research tool. Besides committee reports, ongoing debates, and other documents, the *Record* includes annual reports from various committee chairs, in this instance the House Committee on Indian Affairs. It contains numerous references and cross-references not only to this committee but also to the various Indigenous tribes on whose behalf the committee considered, drafted, and debated bills such as the one at issue here. The Hein online database makes searching through the *Congressional Record* a much easier process for the researcher. See, for example, 69th Cong., 1st Session, Senate, *Hearing on S. 3185*, April 1926; *Congressional Record* for May and June 1926; 70th Cong., 2d Sess., House, Document 493, "Message from the President of the United States Transmitting a Memorandum . . . ," December 22, 1928.

Although Calvin Coolidge supposedly destroyed the great bulk of his presidential papers in 1929, his former secretary preserved a small remnant of them, and the resulting microfilm collection can be examined in the Library of Congress Manuscripts Division. One reel in particular, #115, contains a number of letters related to the origins of the litigation that became the pocket veto case. See March 20 and 21, July 6 and 8, and

October 18 and 23, 1925. While this author was unable to locate any papers of William Lewis, attorney for the Okanogan tribe, the papers of an associate who worked with him on the pocket veto case have been preserved online. See the John G. Carter Papers in Merrill G. Burlinghame Special Collections, Montana State University–Bozeman Library. Carter also participated in a number of other lawsuits filed on behalf of Indigenous tribes. Many such records and documents from them are preserved here, as are multiple examples of Indigenous culture that Carter collected.

Part II: Secondary Sources

For well over a century, histories of Indigenous American tribes have proliferated, with no indication of any abatement. Over the years they have generally been characterized by a synthesis of accusatory, investigatory, and hortatory tendencies. Perhaps the earliest such volume was that published by Helen Hunt Jackson in 1881, *A Century of Dishonor*, and still widely available. More than a century later, at least two outstanding general histories of Native Americans have been completed. See Alexandra Harmon's *Reclaiming the Reservation: Histories of Indian Sovereignty Suppressed and Renewed* (2019). In it, Harmon confronts the question of Indigenous sovereignty, an issue that William Lewis had been prepared to raise in his case on behalf of the Okanogan tribe. Of course the fact that he was unable to do so in no way lessens the significance of his claim. Harmon demonstrates that many historians have taken the position that Indigenous tribes somehow created the problems inherent in nineteenth- and twentieth-century Native American history. In fact, non-Natives have consistently been the cause of such conflicts. These disputes have been generated by an ongoing neocolonialist system that thus far has failed to resolve this critical challenge of Indigenous sovereignty, where it begins and ends, and exactly what it includes. Implicit throughout Harmon's study is the question whether or not a real Indigenous sovereignty can even exist, let alone be compatible, in such a system.

See also David Treuer (Ojibwe), *The Heartbeat of Wounded Knee: Native America from 1890 to the Present* (2019). In exploring this history, Treuer concludes that presenting such an account in fact reveals American history as well. All the issues posed at the founding of our country in 1787, he writes, have been replicated in our treatment of the Native Americans. Rich in bibliographic materials, taken together these books by Harmon and Treuer offer the interested student a superb general introduction to Native American history. See also the AHR Exchange: "Historians and Native American and Indigenous Studies," 125 *American Historical Review* 2 (2020), and the AHR Roundtable: Ned Blackhawk, "The Iron Cage of Erasure: American Indian Sovereignty in Jill Lepore's *These Truths*," 125 *American Historical Review* 5 (2020). Both of these sources are rich in reference citations.

Two other older works, both published under federal auspices, should also be mentioned. The most thorough description of contemporary American tribal life after World War I but before World War II is found in Lewis Meriam's massive study, *The Problem of Indian Administration* (1928). Ruthlessly objective for its day, this detailed critique of contemporary Indigenous tribes' conditions was published by the Institute for Government Research on the eve of the Great Depression. Meriam's coauthors found wide variance in the quality of federal Indian service: "The worst often falls far below the normal." Also see the equally expansive *Handbook of Federal Indian Law*, published in 1942 through the Department of the Interior and edited by Felix Cohen. A critical assessment concerning some negative results from the legislation detailed by Cohen may be found in Walter Echo-Hawk, *In the Courts of the Conqueror: The Ten Worst Indian Law Cases Ever Decided* (2021). In a similar vein, see David Wilkins, *Hollow Justice: A History of Indigenous Claims in the United States* (2013).

The context in which the 1926 statute for the Okanogan was enacted is best understood by an examination of the 1920s. See Randolph Downes, "A Crusade for Reform," 32 *Mississippi Valley Historical Review* (1945). Downes points to the increasing number of congressional statutes passed on behalf of the Indigenous tribes during this decade. See also the same author's *The Rise of Warren Gamaliel Harding, 1865–1920* (1970). This study covers Harding's career to his election as president in 1920. See Eugene Trani and David Wilson, *The Presidency of Warren G. Harding* (1977). Yet the standard work on the Harding presidency remains that of Robert K. Murray, *The Politics of Normalcy: Governmental Theory and Practice in the Harding-Coolidge Era* (1973). For a different perspective that is interesting to read if not totally persuasive, see Francis Russell, *The Shadow of Blooming Grove: Warren G. Harding in His Times* (1968). For the Coolidge presidency, see Robert H. Ferrell, *The Presidency of Calvin Coolidge* (1998). One of the original "muckraker" journalists, William Allen White published an absorbing account of Coolidge's career in his *A Puritan in Babylon: The Story of Calvin Coolidge* (1938). Of related interest is Arthur Link, "What Happened to the Progressive Movement in the 1920s?," 64 *American Historical Review* (1959).

For an understanding of the continuing legal questions concerning the pocket veto that are still relevant to the points William Lewis had hoped to argue on behalf of the Okanogan tribe, see the following sources: "The Presidential Veto Power: A Shallow Pocket," 70 *Michigan Law Review* (1971); Edward Kennedy, "Congress, the President, and the Pocket Veto," 63 *Virginia Law Review* (1977); and Theodore Olson, "The Pocket Veto: Historical Practice and Judicial Precedent," *Memorandum Opinion for the Counsel to the President*, https://www.justice.gov/sites/default/files/olc/legacy/2014/01/29/op-olc-06.pdf (1982).

Congress, 6, 8; court-packing plan and, 127

Congressional Globe, 19

Congressional Record, 30, 54

constitutional construction, 96, 97, 98, 118, 123

Constitutional Convention (1787), 71

constitutional duties, 89, 97, 99, 147

constitutional interpretation, 119, 125

constitutional law, 107, 140, 143

constitutional rights, 74, 82–83, 122

Continental Congress, 117

Cooley, Thomas, 88

Coolidge, Calvin, 29, 40, 41, 45, 49, 51, 61, 63, 74, 77, 81, 82, 84, 86, 87, 93, 106–107, 126, 155; adjournment and, 92, 112; approval from, 43; Indian Citizenship Act and, 30; Lewis and, 44, 47–48, 156; nomination by, 107; pocket veto and, 29, 34–35, 38–39, 47, 56, 57, 61, 69, 70, 73, 75, 85, 88, 93, 94, 150–151; S. 3185 and, 46, 112

Court of Appeals for the District of Columbia Circuit, 137, 138, 139–140, 142, 145, 146, 148, 153

Court of Claims, 4, 9, 10, 16, 20, 31, 34, 37, 38, 40, 43, 48, 49, 50, 52, 55, 56, 79, 81, 82, 83, 85, 86, 88, 90, 94, 108, 113, 116, 118, 120; access to, 26; adjudication by, 25; amendments and, 18; appeal to, 28–29, 30; arguments in, 76, 156; bill for, 7, 14, 15; errors by, 115; establishment of, 5–6, 11–12, 151; finality for, 18, 19; jurisdiction of, 17; lawsuit in, 26, 114, 150, 155, 156; number of judges for, 20, 23, 24; petition with, 57, 65, 69, 78; Shoshones and, 53; strengthening, 7–8, 17, 23; veto power and, 65; vote on, 22; *Wright* and, 114

court-packing plan, 127

Cowlitz tribe, 57

Cramton, Louis, 37, 38, 51, 54–55

Daugherty, Harry, 105, 106

Declaration of Independence, 3

demurrer, 49, 69, 70, 72, 76, 78, 86, 150, 156

Department of Agriculture, 64

Department of the Interior, 26, 27, 40, 51, 52

Department of the Treasury, 5, 35

Diven, Alexander, 9, 11, 12

Downes, Randolph, 30

Echo-Hawk, Walter, 150

Eighth Circuit Court of Appeals, 104

El Salvador, 141, 145, 147

executive authority, 48, 72, 146

Executive Branch, 85, 89, 147; Legislative Branch and, 83, 143

executive department, 6, 17, 50, 54, 152

Fall, Albert, 30

Family Practice of Medicine Act, 133

Federal District Court for the District of Columbia, 106, 133

Federal Employee Liability Act, 104

Fessenden, William Pitt, 16, 20–21, 22; amendment by, 18, 19, 23

Fillmore, Millard, 46

First Amendment, 31, 155

fishing rights, 29, 31

Ford, Gerald R., 139, 140, 157

Fort Bridger Treaty (1868), 52

Foster, Lafayette, 21

Fourteenth Amendment, 11, 15

Galloway, Herman J., 71, 72

Garfield, James, 46

General Accounting Office, 32
George III, 3
Graham, Charles, 62
Grant, Ulysses S., 26, 42, 155
Grimes, James, 19, 20, 21

Hadley, Lindley, 43
Hale, John, 16, 18, 20, 22; Court of
    Claims and, 15, 19; H.R. 226 and, 23;
    Trumbull and, 15, 21
Hamlin, Hannibal, amendments and,
    19, 21
Harding, Warren, 81, 103, 106; appoint-
    ments by, 105; scandals of, 30
Harlan, James, 19, 22
Harlan, John Marshall, 70
Harreld, J., 36
Harrison, Benjamin, 70, 94
Harrison, William Henry, 46
Harvard Law Reform, 106
Hickman, John, 12
Hill, Samuel, 31, 37, 40–41, 43–44, 57;
    Colville Reservation and, 42
Holmes, Oliver Wendell, 103, 104, 105,
    106, 107; Brandeis and, 102; Stone
    and, 102
Homestead Land Grant Act, 23
Hoover, Herbert, 90, 107;
    nominations by, 113
House Budget Committee, 62
House Committee of the Whole, 21,
    51, 112
House Committee on Claims, 5, 120
House Committee on Indian Affairs,
    27, 36, 37, 38, 54
House Committee on the Judiciary,
    19, 63, 64, 81, 92, 96, 100, 122;
    decision from, 62; H.R. 226 and,
    16; H.R. 5218 and, 61; pocket veto
    and, 83, 132; reporting out from, 111;
    Sumners and, 95

House of Representatives, 7, 10, 12, 29,
    39, 94, 151; H.R. 226 and, 14, 24
House Subcommittee on Indian
    Affairs, 27, 30, 38, 40, 41, 51, 52, 155;
    report by, 36; testimony to, 32–35
H.R. 226, 9, 10, 14, 15; amendments
    for, 21–22; debating, 16; delay for,
    19, 21, 22; signing of, 23
H.R. 4042, 141, 146, 147
H.R. 5218, 61, 62, 63, 65
H.R. 9160, 28, 29, 40
H.R. 9270, 29–30, 31, 36, 37, 51
H.R. 13492, 51
Hughes, Charles Evans, 121, 124,
    125–126, 136; pocket veto and, 122,
    132; Roosevelt and, 16, 126; *Wright*
    and, 113, 123, 138, 151
Hughes Court, 131–132
hunting rights, 29, 30, 31

Indian Bureau, 37
Indian Citizenship Act (1924), 30, 155
Indian Department, 54
Indian Office, 27
Indian Reform, 30
Indian War (1855–1858), 32
Indigenous tribes, 17, 26, 31, 36,
    57, 75, 84, 149; antagonism
    toward, 18; cases brought by, 24;
    compensation for, 33; dealing with,
    34; management of, 30; pocket
    veto case and, 150; settlers and, 32

Jackson, Thomas, 141–142, 143
Jefferson, Thomas, 46
Johnson, Andrew, 11
Jones, Wesley, 45, 46
"Judges' Bill" (1925), 84
Justice Department, 93, 106, 157;
    demurrer and, 69; Kennedy and,
    134, 140; motion by, 69–70

Okanogan . . . Indians et al. v. United
 States (1928), 76
Okanogan tribe, 26, 27, 28, 30, 42, 44,
 47, 52, 78, 81, 84, 98; grievances of,
 41, 69, 72; legislation for, 49, 55, 57,
 61; property rights of, 31; suit by, 29
Olsen, Theodore, 140
Ordinance Department, 113

Pacific Railroad Bill, 23
Pendleton, George, 11, 12, 13–14
pocket veto: absoluteness of,
 47; adjournment and, 75,
 85–86, 89, 91, 92, 93, 116, 117, 141;
 constitutional construction for,
 75, 79; constitutionality of, 132,
 151; decision on, 113, 127, 131, 133;
 executive authority and, 151;
 impact of, 97; interpretation of,
 113; intersession, 140; intrasession,
 139, 140; legal objection to,
 74; misinterpretation of, 101;
 ratification of, 150; and regular
 veto compared, 47; responding to,
 50–51; use of, 46, 73–74, 80, 83, 96,
 98, 100, 116, 120, 121, 126, 137, 140–141
Poole, Rufus, 26–27
Porter, Albert, 8–9; bill by, 10, 12, 14,
 16–17, 19, 23, 24; H.R. 226 and, 9, 11
Powell, Lazarus, 18
Powell, Lewis, 143
power: constitutional, 74, 82–83,
 124; judicial, 136; legislative, 89;
 separation of, 143, 151–152. *See also*
 veto power
"Primus inter Pares," 103

Raker, John, 41, 57
Reagan, Ronald, pocket veto and,
 141, 157

recess, 73, 80, 120, 123–124
Recess Appointments Clause, 152
Reconstruction, 46
Reed, Stanley, 115–116
Reeder, Robert, 85, 93, 94, 112
Rehnquist, William, 147, 148
Report on the Pocket Veto, 84, 85
Revolutionary War, 4
 rights and claims, 68
rights and privileges, 68
Roberts, Owen J., *Wright* and, 113
Robinson, Spottswood, 142
Roosevelt, Franklin D., 104, 114, 117,
 119, 121; appointments by, 113; court-
 packing plan and, 127; pocket veto
 and, 114, 116, 123–124, 151, 157; *Wright*
 and, 126–127, 132
Roosevelt, Theodore, 102, 104

S. 713, 115, 117, 121
S. 1480, 56
S. 3185, 38, 40, 45, 46, 68, 73, 76, 77, 90,
 91, 92, 95, 100; implementing, 65;
 pocket veto of, 51, 70, 75, 78
S. 3418, 133, 138, 139; veto of, 137
S. 4611, reporting out of, 51–52
Sanford, Edward, 100, 102,
 107–108, 110, 112, 116, 122, 123,
 125; adjournment and, 108, 111;
 appointment of, 106; findings of,
 126, 132; Mitchell and, 109; opinion
 by, 131; pocket veto and, 109, 152
San Poil tribe, 26
Saunders, Everett, 48
Scalia, Antonin, 145
Senate, 11, 15, 17, 19, 22, 29, 30, 142, 151;
 H.R. 226 and, 20, 21, 24; Porter bill
 and, 14
Senate Committee on Claims, 114,
 118, 124

veto clause, 118, 126; purpose of, 74, 90
vetoes: absolute, 82, 87, 88, 97;
 overriding, 91, 134; using, 46, 120
veto power, 45, 87, 88, 117, 144;
 constitutional provisions of, 65;
 protecting, 126; using, 119–120

Waddy, Joseph, 134–135, 137, 138; *Wright*
 and, 136
War of 1812, 4
Washington State, 25, 26, 32, 40, 41, 56,
 67, 68, 84; reservation land in, 255
Washington State Bar, 27
Watergate crisis, 139, 140
Whitaker, Sam, S. 713 and, 118
White, Edward, 103, 184
Wiecek, William, 3, 5
Williams, Ashby, 118; on

adjournment, 115; recess and,
 116–117
Williamson, William, 40, 52, 53
Wilson, Woodrow, 81, 104, 105
Wood, William, 61–62, 63, 65
Work, Hubert, 27, 29, 30, 51
Wright, David, 113, 118, 156; arguments
 by, 124; petition by, 114–115, 157
Wright, Hendrik, 13–14
Wright v. United States (1938), 113, 114,
 120, 123, 124, 126, 126–127, 131–132, 137,
 138, 142, 144, 149, 151, 157; questions
 from, 115; reasoning in, 136;
 reliance on, 136
writ of certiorari, 82, 84, 114, 115, 16,
 145, 156, 157

Yakima War, 42, 67